SHARP

Simple Strategies to Boost Your Brainpower

By Heidi Hanna, PhD

ISBN (for hardcover edition): 978-0-9836127-5-9
ISBN (for paperback edition): 978-0-9836127-7-3

PRAISE FOR *SHARP: SIMPLE STRATEGIES TO BOOST YOUR BRAINPOWER*

"Truly motivational! Dr. Hanna provides practical brain prescriptions that really work to change your life. Backed by scientific evidence, personal heartfelt guidance, and professional experience, this practical guide is a must-read for everyone who is seeking to optimize brainpower! I loved it. So will you."

Ann Louise Gittleman, PhD, CNS,
NY Times Bestselling Author of *The Fat Flush Plan*

"We all know that stress is killing us and damaging our companies and relationships – Heidi Hanna's landmark book, *SHARP*, offers concise, intelligent ways to do something specific – now – to reduce our stress levels. This book is stuffed with valuable insights, realistic advice, and serious programs; from my perspective as a cognitive psychologist, Heidi's text is not only a must-read – for higher health, success, and happiness, it's a must-do!"

John Selby, Author of *Executive Genius*

"What I love about *SHARP* is the comprehensive approach to health, happiness, and performance of mind and body. We all know we can do better with our nutrition, exercise, and mental health, but time and execution prevent many of us from being the best we can be. I am a big proponent of *SHARP*, and believe if you have any desire to get change in gear, this is the way to go. It is simple, sustainable, and will change your life. It changed mine."

Larry Milder, National Sales Director, Legg Mason

"For us business people, 10 percent of our time drives 90 percent of our productivity ... What Dr. Hanna has done here is show us how to make that 10 percent of time perform magnificently."

John Evans, Executive Director, Janus Labs

"Dr. Heidi Hanna draws you in with her fascinating stories and realistic approach to improving your brain's fitness. Her "Fab 5" strategies are doable and easy to implement, even for the busiest of people. From ways to tweak your diet to learning to relax and create emotional connections, *SHARP* is jam-packed with useful nuggets of must-do methods to boost brain power and feel happier!"

Tara Gidus, MS, RD, Team Dietician for the Orlando Magic NBA Team,
Author of *Pregnancy Cooking and Nutrition for Dummies*

"Take this doctor's orders and read *SHARP*! As Hanna points out, cognitive exercises for the brain are as important as aerobic activity is for the body. This is one visit to the mental gym you won't want to skip!"

Marshall Goldsmith, Author of *Mojo* and
What Got You Here Won't Get You There

"Dr. Heidi Hanna has created an accessible and friendly doorway for her readers into the often complex and confusing world of modern science and "brainpower!" In easy-to-understand and practical terms, in this book, she shows readers how to build on the good news of modern science about the brain's capacity to change and the power of exercise, nutrition, and self-awareness to promote health and well-being. Any reader interested in boosting their own brainpower and happiness should find something useful here!"

Dr. Jeffery Brantley, Director of Mindfulness Based
Stress Reduction – Duke Integrative Medicine

"A must-read for anyone with a brain, this book is liberally punctuated with real-world applications that are immediately useful and do-able. Dr. Hanna has raised the bar for books on brain health with a resource that is not merely a collection of interesting information (which it indeed is!), but a transformational and invaluable tool for life."

Theresa Robinson, President, Corporate Trainer,
and Performance Coach - Master Trainer TMR & Associates, LLC

"*SHARP* is a great book for anyone who wants to learn how to take control of their lifestyle and enjoy more in their mental and physical health. It's simple, practical, written in a very user-friendly way, whilst at the same time providing you with some key insights into modern brain science and the field of health. Heidi Hanna's passion for helping people comes through in every chapter of the book, and by the time you have read *SHARP* you'll feel equipped with the essential information you need to succeed. A great read!"

Justin Buckthorp, PGA European Tour Medical Advisory Board

"Heidi Hanna has delivered a revealing and relevant system to achieve great results. This is a book that needs to be read and re-read because it is packed with practical tips and strategies that can impact your personal and business bottom line. If you're ready for a real breakthrough, order your copy today!"

Derrick Kinney, Senior Financial Advisor – Ameriprise Financial

DEDICATION

This book is dedicated to
the millions of caregivers who unconditionally love and
support those with Alzheimer's disease
and other forms of dementia.

While we continue to work hard to find a cure,
may we all live a life that enables us to be
as healthy and happy as possible,
right here and now.

Bringing not only more years to our life,
but more life to our years.

50% of all book proceeds will be donated to
the Alzheimer's Association

CONTENTS

ACKNOWLEDGMENTS

Many people dream of writing a book, but for me...well, I always dreamed of writing an acknowledgments page. Seriously. I would sit up late at night thinking about all the people I wanted to thank for my journey before I had a clue where it would actually lead me. I am overwhelmingly inspired by my family, friends, and the clients I've had the opportunity to get to know along the way. Your stories of perseverance and bravery push me to do whatever it takes to continue this work. I am truly grateful!

First and foremost to my incredible family. Dad, thank you for being my #1 fan and the best coach in the world. You taught me from a very early age to dream big, and believed in me even when I didn't believe in myself. Mom, you're my rock. Thank you for always keeping me grounded and reminding me that I am loved, unconditionally. To my brother, Tony, and his wife, Willow, thank you for demonstrating to me what it means to be truly dedicated parents and for bringing me the two most special kids in my life, Brady and Lexi. And to my 'bonus mom,' Jami, thank you for being brave enough to open the blinds for me from time to time.

To my second family at *SYNERGY*, especially Jacquelyn Mack, thank you for holding me accountable and being so passionate about our shared mission. To my research assistant, Stephanie Matos, thank you for your hard work and dedication to quality.

To the 'pioneers' in my career, Chris Osorio, Dana Klein, and Trevor Lauer, thank you for believing in me and for your continued guidance and encouragement, especially early on. To my amazing mentors, Dr. Jim Loehr and Dr. Jack Groppel, I feel honored to have learned from the best and hope that I continue to make you proud.

To my 'sole sisters' and Team In Training teammates Robin Grasso, Andrea Canny, and Colleen Legge, thank you for your support and friendship. To my 'counselor on the run,' Kristine Entwistle for listening to me go on and on and on during our training runs and races and for always being a fantastic sounding board and friend.

To my friends at Janus, including the sales directors around the US and the globe – and especially the Janus Labs team, including Tracy Thomas and John Evans – thank you for your continued encouragement and support.

To the colleagues I've had the honor and privilege of working with along the way – especially Theresa Robinson, Tara Gidus, Bill McAlpine, George Dom, Admiral Ray Smith, and Ron Woods – thank you for inspiring me with your gifts of excellence in teaching and coaching. Thank you to Randy Glasbergen for helping me to laugh more, and allowing me to use his fabulous comics in this book, and to my writing coach Adam Martin. To my editor, John Selby – thank you for your major contributions and for your guidance in helping me live what I teach throughout this adventure.

HOW TO USE THIS BOOK

In order to make this book as thorough and beneficial as possible, I created an interactive version that includes video and audio tracks, which is available as an iBook on the apple website. As a reader of the print version of this book, I wanted to give you the opportunity to have the same interactive experience, which is why I have included QR Codes for various learning tools such as video explanations, guided relaxation tracks and other tools. You can scan the QR code using a free QR scanner on your Smartphone, or you can also access these materials by going to www.synergyprograms. com/sharptools.

Each QR code will take you directly to the learning tool,
or if you want to access all of the tools on one page you can
scan the QR code below

NOTE TO READER

The information made available through *SYNERGY* and the book *SHARP: Simple Strategies to Boost Your Brainpower* is not intended to replace the services of a physician. Content in this book and on our website is provided for informational purposes only and is not a substitute for professional medical advice. You should not use the information from this program for diagnosing or treating a medical or health condition. Please consult a physician on all matters relating to your health, particularly with respect to any symptoms that may require diagnosis or medical attention. Before implementing any changes to your nutrition and fitness regimen, talk with your doctor. Obtain medical clearance before beginning an exercise program.

Any action in response to the information provided in this book is at the reader's discretion. The author and publisher have checked with sources believed to be reliable in their efforts to provide information that is complete and generally in accord with the standards accepted at the time of publication. However, in view of the possibility of human error or changes in medical sciences, neither the author nor the publisher nor any other party who has been involved in the preparation or publication of this work warrants that the information contained herein is in every respect accurate or complete, and they are not responsible for any errors or omissions or for the results obtained from the use of such information.

SYNERGY and the book *SHARP: Simple Strategies to Boost Your Brainpower* make no representations or warranties with respect to any information offered or provided on or through the program materials regarding treatment, action, or application of medication, and are not liable for any direct or indirect claim, loss, or damage resulting from use of this book or any websites linked from it.

INTRODUCTION
Beyond System Overload

There is much talk in the American workplace about new brain-exercise programs that promise to raise mental performance to higher and higher levels. Most of these 'revolutionary' programs encourage people to set aside time to push themselves through ever more challenging mental tasks designed to sharpen various aspects of brain activity. However, much has happened during the last few years, especially in medical and psychological understandings of how the brain works, and what the brain needs most in order to perform at peak levels, day in and day out.

With so much mental pressure and stress continually pressing in on you at work, the truth is you don't necessarily need to do **more** things in order to be sharper mentally – you need to **do things smarter.**

In this book, we'll review scientific research, and delve into the new wisdom regarding how you can manage your brain and body in order to become truly super fit and sharp, even when running on high speed at work or at home.

You'll find this book full of medical and psychological studies that have awakened us to a new vision of cognitive fitness. You'll also see in these pages an innovative power approach to brain fitness, designed to not only improve your mental energy and performance, but also enhance your ability to manage stress while boosting your health and happiness.

When you finish this book, you will not only be highly informed, but also in possession of a core daily exercise routine that can truly transform both your personal and professional life.

Cognitive fitness is in many ways very similar to physical fitness, and it's important to know how to exercise your 'mental muscles' properly if you want to keep sharp. However, there are certain ways in which cognitive fitness and peak mental performance require a unique approach, in order to actively reduce the effects of chronic work stress on both your body and your brain.

Only when you gain this new view of the relationship between stress and performance, and act accordingly, can you shift purposefully into a higher level of cognitive clarity, innovation, health, happiness, and longevity.

To see a video of author Heidi Hanna talking about 'system overload,' scan the QR code below

The New Vision of Fitness

Even in physical fitness, it's clear that non-stop strenuous exercise is not the best approach to being strong, coordinated, and healthy. Regular periods of rest and recovery are required at all levels of biological dynamics in order for your muscles to develop and function optimally. And when it comes to your mental energy, this regular conscious oscillation between exercise and rest is especially important – both as something to understand, and also to regularly practice.

In other words, science has now documented that it's **critical not to over-train your brain**; instead, you need to train strategically in ways that will actively reduce stress, encourage neural expansion, and help your brain regularly recover and express its full potential.

It's important to remember that fitness, both physical and mental, isn't just about brute strength. Yes, you do need to keep your brain fit for bouts of long hours dealing with a mass of detail – that's part of work. But there are three dimensions to mental fitness: strength, flexibility, and endurance.

To nurture these three intertwined brain qualities, sometimes you need to actively engage your mind in cognitive workouts – but from time to time you also need to shift into recovery mode for creative insight.

And at work, just like at home, you also need to be able to instantly shift into interpersonal empathy mode, so that you can relate with your team or clients at highly successful levels.

Work Stress versus Cognitive Fitness

There's no way of getting around the blunt fact that work usually generates mental stress – and a stressed-out brain performs at progressively lower levels. Stress is without question the number one killer of both efficiency and creativity. In this light, it's vital to learn specific ways to regularly shift your focus of attention out of stress mode and into rest mode at work, so that your chronically deep-fried synapses have at least a few 'time-out' moments during the day to regroup, recover, and recharge.

At first you might react negatively to the idea of having to set aside regular down time for your brain. You're already feeling pressured by deadlines, and taking time off seems counterproductive to getting things done. But just the opposite will prove to be the case. Consider the concept of muscle fatigue: Without short breaks from physical stress, your muscles at some point will begin to spasm and malfunction. Periodic rest is required for the system to repair and become stronger.

As we'll see from medical studies, the same basic thing happens in your brain. You begin to lose the mental power necessary to hold your focus on your work, causing more errors and less creative vitality.

Focus is what work is all about. Your attention, like your energy, is one of the most valuable resources you possess, and it's important to think deeply about how you are using and managing that resource.

Your mental capacity (strength, flexibility, endurance) drives not only performance, but also your engagement with people who matter to you. And if you personally don't take care of your mental fitness and stay balanced and charged for action, you can't possibly take care of anyone or anything else.

What are you spending on, or paying attention to?

Are you saving any reserves?

Do you have a long-term investment strategy to make sure that you don't run out?

As the flight attendant says before a flight, "Please put your own oxygen mask on before assisting other passengers." I'm not sure if everyone realizes the importance of this statement. It's not just about being good to yourself – if you run out of oxygen, you can't help save anyone else.

Making sure that you take time to keep your own brain sharp is one of the primary responsibilities you carry to work each morning. It's also what you want to preserve so you have energy left at the end of the day to spend with the people and things that matter most to you.

You have most likely already experienced how stress damages cognitive health and performance. In this book we're going to delve fully into 'stress versus brain' issues, and consider the most effective ways to periodically shift out of stress mode altogether in order to recover, rebalance, and recharge our mental energy. These essential breaks will make you feel better, revitalize your performance, and keep your brain resilient over time.

The *SHARP* Brain Recharge Process

Throughout this book, as we explore all the various aspects of brain fitness step by step, you will be gently guided to master one particular brain exercise that will stand at the heart of this discussion – the *SHARP* Brain Recharge.

The format will appear quite simple, and that's just how we want it. The intent of the process isn't to make your brain do more work, since that's most likely the problem in the first place. Just the opposite is needed – a short effective method that enables you to temporarily shift out of work mode altogether for just a few minutes.

Why do this? **Because your brain absolutely needs cognitive downtime in order to function optimally**. But as you know, just taking time out to catch your breath usually doesn't get the brain recovery job done, because your mind is so habituated to going non-stop that it doesn't know how to turn off.

I'll be teaching you my version of this cognitive shifting technique in this book. I can confidently guarantee you that this Brain Recharge will become one of the core assets in your mental energy bank, because it gets the job done fast, providing you with a significant energy return on your time investment.

A three minute Brain Recharge break can give you up to two hours of high charge, high performance action in its wake; that's pure gold in our workplace where you're not usually evaluated just on data punching, but on your higher mental performance, social verve, innovative insight, and overall brightness of mind.

You will find that the Brain Recharge not only quiets your busy, stressed-out mind, it also directly allows you to feel good in your physical body in the present moment. This in turn raises your overall mood, and boosts the energy you exude to others, so that when you return your focus to the work at hand, your overall stress is down and your health profile is raised up.

The underlying idea here is not to train harder, but to train smarter. Similar to a muscle, the brain needs to be used regularly in order to keep up its conditioning. But also similar to a muscle, if you're not strategic about how you train, you can find yourself constantly breaking down instead of building up.

Too much mental training leads to 'overuse injuries' such as fatigue, distraction, slow processing, cellular atrophy, and subtle brain damage. When you are able to give yourself moments of mental recovery, you directly reduce the symptoms of overuse, and also begin to treat the core cause of stress and mental malfunction.

Consciously Feeding Your Brain

Your body knows how to restore balance, or homeostasis, if only you give it a chance. The Brain Recharge process will teach you how to accomplish this important goal.

Studies consistently show that when chronic stress, worry, or anxiety generates an imbalance in your system, your brain is unable to operate efficiently. Shifting your attention temporarily toward present moment positive feelings enables the internal balance to be regained at respiratory, biological, and emotional levels, and thus you feel more collaborative, creative, and hopeful.

The key to quickly recovering proper oxygenation in the brain (and throughout the body) is to momentarily set your breathing free, not to try to control it more tightly through forced deep breathing. When your brain is in a positive, balanced state, you can perform at your best and keep your operating system flexible.

Your personal energy is not a limitless resource. In order to keep your brain functioning at its best over time, you must strategically invest energy back into it. You can do this purposefully by focusing your attention regularly toward demonstrating more wisdom, compassion, and support for your own health and satisfaction in life.

Five Fundamentals of Brain Health

The Brain Recharge process is the first step toward creating a new positive habit of maintaining top condition mentally, emotionally, and physically. By practicing this short method three times a day at work, you will quickly boost your energy across each dimension.

We will also be exploring a set of five *SHARP* fundamentals that will reinforce and expand the Brain Recharge dimension of this program. I'll help you look carefully at your current behaviors – the food you eat, your movement habits, your overall approach to stress, your sleep habits, and your sense of social connection – and identify what science recommends on all five fronts. We'll also consider how you can maximize your health and vitality by developing special cognitive fitness exercises and routines.

Keep in mind, the same principles that will keep you mentally sharp in the present moment are also recommended for keeping you healthy later in life, and may reduce the risk of dementia and Alzheimer's disease.

The fundamentals in this *SHARP* program will give your genetic makeup the best opportunity to stay bright and healthy. You can't change your genes, but you can alter how they are expressed, and therefore positively impact your longevity outcome.

In Sum

At deeper levels, I want to encourage you to see as clearly as possible that simple choices regarding how you manage your mind carry ultimate power to determine how your life unfolds. I also hope to share with you how the seemingly small self-care practices you employ today will seriously make a difference in your health, happiness, and performance, now... and into the future.

How can a busy, talented person like you become more healthy, fulfilled, and effective? The key word is focus: don't let your calendar run you – you run your calendar. Block off time each day to work out mentally, to take Brain Recharge Breaks, and implement the simple strategies of the *SYNERGY* Fab 5 to support a healthy brain foundation.

If you run your life like you're the CEO of your own domain, even within the confines of your organization, you'll optimize all aspects of your life.

"No, I don't think you're crazy. Like most of us, you're just a victim of bad programming."

PART ONE

The Brain: Your Operating System

CHAPTER 1
Genuine Cognitive Fitness

What does it really mean to be cognitively fit? When we use the word 'fitness' we are usually referring to physical fitness, or the capacity to do work. The most commonly used definition of physical fitness comes from the U.S. Department of Health & Human Services: "Physical fitness is a set of attributes that people have or achieve relating to their ability to perform a physical activity."

The requirements of health-related physical fitness are 1) strength, 2) flexibility, and 3) cardiovascular fitness, or endurance. Good trainers always clarify that in order to be physically fit, all three aspects need to be developed and maintained through regular training.

So then, what does it take to be *cognitively fit*?
Not surprisingly, the components are quite similar.

To see a video of author Heidi Hanna talking about cognitive fitness, scan the QR code below

Enhanced Performance

Everyone is looking for an edge to help them perform better and stand out from the competition. With only so much time and energy, how do we make ourselves as *SHARP* as possible so we can perform at our best, be positive and resilient, and stay focused on what is most important to us?

Researchers in the fields of neuroscience, psychology, and physiology have demonstrated that brain training exercises can have both immediate and long-term effects when practiced regularly.[1,2,3] And this conclusion couldn't come at a better time, as the strain on mental energy is at an all-time high.

We also now know that taking short, scheduled breaks from mental work to temporarily shift out of cognitive-stress mode altogether can quickly refresh the brain's performance power.

Times have changed radically at work, and yet our minds continue to operate within a fairly old-fashioned system. For instance, people used to focus primarily on one thing at a time as their job assignment; but now we are expected to do more with less as our current chaotic environment is filled with distractions, causing us to multitask constantly.

Even though our job description often insists we are proficient at multitasking, research has clearly demonstrated that multitasking is not a skill to be developed, but rather a bad habit that needs to be eliminated.

Numerous studies have demonstrated that chronic multitasking slows us down, and dumbs us down, as we spread our attention in multiple directions at once.[4,5,6] Yet, even though the negative impact of multitasking has been well documented, we continue to multitask too much of the time because we've trained our brain to automatically attempt to work that way. Part of cognitive fitness is based on our ability to manage our focus of attention and pay attention to one task at a time, so that we do our best at that task.

Realistically, most of us will need some cognitive re-training in order to remember the fine art of staying focused on one thing at a time. Part of your cognitive fitness program will include these re-training exercises.

Just knowing in theory that you *should* do something (such as focus on one task at a time) has never been the solution. It takes discipline and practice to shift out of multitasking habits into single-minded focusing at work.

I love what Rick Hanson says about multitasking in his book *Buddha's Brain*:

> *"Multitasking is the art of distracting yourself from two*
> *separate things you'd rather not be doing,*
> *by doing them simultaneously."*[7]

One of the main complaints I hear from my clients is the chronic sense of feeling overwhelmed at work – especially when multitasking. Research shows that this condition of mental overload leads predictably to decreased productivity and reduced engagement in the workplace. It's estimated that 'disengaged' employee time costs US businesses $300 billion every year due to errors, lower productivity, absenteeism, turnover, and accidents.[8]

We are without question hired to perform, and how we manage our own mind determines to a large degree our performance

level. Cognitive fitness needs to address the root factors that help us perform at higher levels, both for our company's success and also for our own inner sense of self esteem and work fulfillment.

There are five primary whole-body health factors that support or undermine our mental performance levels. I call these the '*SYNERGY Fab 5*', and we'll be exploring how you can positively improve all five factors in your life and work. The impact of this improvement will not only help you succeed at higher levels, but also feel more healthy and happy with your life in general.

Improved Resilience

In addition to compromising performance, ever-increasing time pressures at work also generate a chronic stress pattern that is damaging to your brain's vitality and resilience.

Under-managed stress in the American work environment progressively drains your brain in terms of nutrients and overall 'spring-back' capacity, so that you experience fatigue and burn-out too often at work. And when you finish work, you feel dull mentally, low emotionally, and unable to enjoy your personal life.

According to the 2008 'State of Health in the American Workforce' Survey, one-third of employees report that their work has a primarily negative impact on their lives off the job. Because constant mental stress drains their energy, they report not having enough energy left over for their personal or family life.[9]

At work we continue to do more with less, as businesses cut back support staff, increase minimum production levels, reduce compensation structures, and so on. The toll that this everyday stress takes on our body, mind, and spirit has been well documented, as we will continue to discuss throughout this book, and something must be done to reverse the situation.

There are simple choices you can make, each day, to improve and maintain your mental resilience. Taking personal responsibility for the flexibility of your brain, so that you're able to spring back into mental sharpness after challenging brainwork, is one of the vital outcomes that we'll focus on in this discussion.

Successful Aging

Along with chronic busyness and debilitating stress at work, we all know that we aren't getting any younger. This means we get to deal with the negative age-related factors that develop within our brains. As we continue to extend our lifespan through advances in science and medicine, diseases that are related to aging become more and more epidemic.

This year marks a turning point for our large baby boomer populatio. It's the first year that this generation starts to turn 65, the approximate age when the risk of developing Alzheimer's disease or other forms of dementia begins to increase rapidly. By the age of 85, our risk of having Alzheimer's disease becomes a coin toss.[10]

From 2000-2008, all of the major health issues significantly decreased in scope, except for one – Alzheimer's disease – which increased 68%![11]

Unfortunately, the current high-stress lifestyle most people live only enhances this mental deterioration process. The good news is that researchers are discovering that our fate may be more in our own hands than we once thought.

Healthy living and mental exercise as outlined in this book may boost the number of brain cells we have, the number of connections between cells, the strength of each individual cell and its connections, and the stimulation of brain chemicals that fuel cell growth.

Unfortunately, not enough people are aware of just how much our day-to-day choices impact our life. Both for future mental wellness and present-moment performance, each day we make choices that determine the health of our brains.

A fascinating discovery in Alzheimer's research happened as a result of the now-famous 'nun study'.[12] Upon autopsy, it was found that many of the women who had developed Alzheimer's related plaques and tangles in their brains had shown *no symptoms* of the disease in their later years of life. If you consider what's happening in the brain when you get enough physical and mental exercise, eat right, and include the other healthy habits we'll talk about in the Fab 5, it makes perfect sense that the cognitively and physically fit nuns in the study could remain free from Alzheimer's symptoms.

With more cells being created regularly, and with more and stronger connections, there are more options for the brain to

communicate and function successfully, despite obstacles that might otherwise get in the way as a result of damage, disease, or just regular aging.

Considering that I have had three grandparents diagnosed with Alzheimer's, this finding caught my attention (and prompted an e-mail to my family members hoping to encourage and motivate them to take action with their own choices regarding their health).

In essence, the question comes down to this: we may be living longer, but are we living better? Dan Buettner, the author of *Blue Zones*, said this perfectly:

> *"It's not just about adding more years to your life,*
> *but adding more life to your years."*[13]

With the right cognitive fitness training program, you can extend your life and stay healthier longer, allowing you to do successful mental work throughout the aging process, and to enjoy your time to the fullest. Again, there is the choice: once you know how to stay fit throughout your life, are you willing to make small changes that enable your brain to perform with extra power and resilience, keeping you healthier and happier now and into the future?

Start with a Healthy Foundation

If you do choose to optimize your brainpower, you will want to start by creating a long-term health foundation on which to build your cognitive fitness program.

Obviously a smoker can't expect to get maximum benefits from a cardiovascular training session (although many people still try), and someone working with an injured muscle can't expect to have an extraordinary strength training workout. You can't expect to get in great shape if you're constantly stopping for fast food.

Similarly, in order for brain training to yield maximum benefit, it's essential to first support your system through healthy whole-body habits that nurture the brain environment and provide optimum energy and nutrients needed to fuel your cognitive fitness.

We will ground our cognitive fitness training program with a discussion of how to promote optimal overall brain health.

The *SYNERGY* Fab 5 will highlight the most important aspects of a healthy lifestyle that directly nurture the health and function of your brain.

By utilizing these strategies, you will create and sustain the best possible environment for your brain, so that you can achieve optimal results from the training routine you implement.

Here are the core elements of the *SYNERGY* Fab 5:

1. Nutrition – Food is Fuel: It's important to eat light and often, to eat a balanced menu, and to eat foods high in nutritional value. I'll introduce a simple, realistic yet powerful approach to a brain healthy diet.

2. Movement – Activity is Activating: I will encourage you to move often throughout the day, to never sit longer than 90 minutes without movement, and to perform aerobic, resistance, and flexibility training regularly.

3. Recovery – Balancing Stress Balances Life: Regular recovery from stress is not an option, it's essential; and for success, self-care must be scheduled. I'll discuss how stress impacts your brain and what you can do to create a healthy balance.

4. Sleep – Resting is Working: Getting a good night's sleep is critical for repairing and rebuilding the brain. Most people require 7-8 hours of restful sleep; if this is an issue for you, we'll explore a bedtime routine that will help you develop more healthy sleep habits.

5. Connection – Social Support is Life Support: Research shows that social isolation is bad for your health and mental performance; you need to regularly pause and perceive that you're connected with a group of friends. We'll talk strategies for expanding social connections if this is a challenge for you.

Cognitive Fitness & Recovery Strategies

As you establish the foundation for boosting your brainpower, you're also ready to begin exercising the brain itself, and to learn special methods to help you rest and recover from brain stress.

In approaching brain exercise, it might help to keep in mind how each element of your cognitive functioning is similar to a dimension of physical fitness.

Mental Strength Training: You can develop mental muscle through a strength building regimen designed to help strengthen the communication pathways in the brain, creating more secure neural connections that enable thoughts to flow through your mind faster and more accurately.

The strength training program discussed in this book consists of specific strategies that help your brain develop stronger neurons, recruit additional neurons for increased speed and accuracy, and improve your resistance to detrimental habits such as associative distraction (drifting into related but non-productive thoughts) and multitasking.

Mental Flexibility Training: Similar to flexibility training for the body, improving mental flexibility develops our ability to be resilient, and to manage stress more effectively so that it enhances rather than hinders our performance. Strategies such as positivity training, initiating the relaxation response, and adapting our mindset help to provide resilience to stress and increase balance in our lives.

Specifically, I will teach you a powerful new way to almost instantly shift temporarily away from stress entirely, into 'relax-rebalance-recharge' mode. We will also discuss the power of positivity, and ways to train your brain to focus more on what's good in your life.

Mental Endurance Training: Like endurance training for the body, which improves the efficiency of our heart and lungs to keep us going over time, mental endurance training requires a similar approach so that you can maintain longevity in mental performance, and also stay healthy throughout the aging process.

This type of training incorporates elements of strength and flexibility in a 'cross training' format for maximum impact. Sustaining performance over time also requires short, consistent recovery breaks that will maximize your brain's sustainability.

Throughout this book I'll be teaching you specific exercises that will help you build a solid program for optimal brainpower, so that by the time you're ready to put a plan into place you'll have already learned the basics of a daily brain fitness program.

Key Principles of Brain Training

When choosing exercises to train your brain, it's important to keep in mind the following principles for improving cognitive fitness, based on the American College of Sports Medicine's physical fitness guidelines, which also apply to improving the fitness of your brain.

1. Make sure it's specific: You would never spend time working out your bicep muscles in order to get bigger calves. In a similar manner, if you want to be more focused, do focusing exercises; if you want to develop a more optimistic outlook, do positivity training; if you want to reduce the effects of stress on your brain, train to quickly initiate the relaxation response.

2. Make sure it's challenging: If you do something you already do well, your brain doesn't have to work at it. In order to stimulate growth, it's important to perform exercises and activities that require effort and even a little discomfort – this stimulates the biological adaptation process that will lead to improvements.

3. Practice it consistently: Remember, just like the muscles in your body, the biochemistry of the brain follows a 'use it or lose it' model. In order to maintain your previous gains and continue to see improvements, it is important to be consistent with your training program and establish lifelong exercise habits.

Where To Begin

In picking up this book, you have already taken the first step toward improving your cognitive health and fitness. You realize that there is something you could be doing a bit differently, potentially better, to maximize your brainpower. You already know you want to strengthen your cognitive abilities and get a greater edge so that you can perform at higher levels.

To help you determine the best starting point for your training, I've included a non-judgmental assessment so that you can start to understand the various parameters of optimum brain fitness, and identify where you want to focus your attention first.

The *SHARP* Assessment

We're going to consider six different dimensions of health, vitality, and performance in this survey. Each of these dimensions is important to your brain's clarity and stamina.

You have the ability, with perhaps some specific guidance and encouragement, to positively change each of these dimensions that you find needs improvement.

Please keep in mind that this is not a test that you pass or fail, but simply an experience to help shed light on your present situation. To get a clear picture of the habits that may be leading you towards, or away from, your goals. As you read through the rest of this book, you'll apply what you discover about yourself to each discussion about how to improve your brainpower.

To see a video of author Heidi Hanna discussing the SHARP Assessment, scan the QR code below

This assessment may also be downloaded in a PDF format at www.synergyprograms.com/sharptools.

#1: Nutrition – *Food is Fuel*

Your ingrained eating habits determine the actual brain fuel that you're taking into your system. These habits are among the most important and most challenging life patterns that can be changed to quickly boost your brainpower.

Check any of the following that are true for you:

___ I usually eat something every 3-4 hours during the day.

___ I usually eat balanced meals and snacks (approximately 25% protein, 25% whole grains, and 50% fruits & veggies at each meal).

___ I very seldom drink more than 2 servings of alcohol a day.

___ I very seldom consume food portions that are larger than what would make me feel physically satisfied.

___ I regularly consume foods with high nutritional value (fruits, veggies, fish and lean protein, nuts, seeds, whole grains).

___ I eat fatty fish at least 1-2 times per week or take a fish oil supplement.

Total "I'm fueling strategically" checks for section #1 ___

#2: Physical Movement – *Activity is Activating*

Life is movement, from our breathing and heartbeat to the circulation of our blood and flow of chemical messages throughout our bodies. But it's so easy to move less and less; to sit for long periods of time due to ever increasing demands on our time and energy. The result is that we become sluggish, our brain receives less than optimum nutrients, our health deteriorates, and we lack the energy we need to perform at our best.

Check any of the following that are true for you:

___ I almost never sit for longer than 90 minutes at one time without standing up or stretching.

___ I usually get at least 60 minutes of general movement activity each day.

___ As weather permits, I go outside for fresh air/sunshine on a daily basis to walk, jog, ride a bicycle, etc.

___ I get at least 20 minutes of moderate-intensity cardiovascular activity a minimum of 3x a week.

___ I do full body strength training exercises a minimum of 2x a week.

___ I stretch regularly after exercise

Total "I'm moving regularly" checks for section #2 ___

#3: Stress Management – *Balanced Stress is Balanced Life*

Stress is part of life for everyone, and a certain amount of stress is good for us. But too much chronic stress is toxic to our system and needs to be balanced by incorporating strategic recovery.

Check any of the following that are true for you:

___ I feel as though I balance my stress levels in a healthy way (not relying on substances like alcohol to calm down).

___ I regularly practice relaxation strategies (meditation, yoga, walking, massage, etc).

___ I very seldom feel highly frustrated, angry, or irritable.

___ I usually feel positive and see challenges as opportunities, rather than feel pessimistic or stuck in 'survival mode.'

___ I usually enjoy challenges at work and do not feel anxious or threatened by failure.

___ When work is over I am able to turn it off and focus on other things.

Total 'I'm relaxing' checks for section #3 ___

#4: Sleep – *Resting is Working*

Your brain requires a certain amount of restful sleep each night if it's going to perform at optimum levels the next day. Over a third of our population suffers from one form or another of insomnia.

Check any of the following that are true for you:

___ I sleep at least 7 hours each night, and usually feel refreshed in the mornings.

___ I do not feel sleepy or lethargic during the day.

___ I usually wake up in the morning when I want to, without setting an alarm clock.

___ Most of the time, without any medication, I fall asleep within 30 minutes of going to bed at night.

___ Usually I sleep soundly throughout the night, or with only one wake-up.

___ Worried and stressful thoughts, memories, and apprehensions seldom interfere with my falling asleep.

Total "I'm resting" checks for section #4 ___

#5: Connection – *Social Support is Life Support*

Many studies have shown that the feeling of being emotionally connected with a group improves our general health and also our performance at work.

Check any of the following that are true for you:

___ I have enough good friends and family connections to feel well connected socially and intimately.

___ I seldom feel isolated or lonely.

___ I have enough emotional connections to feel nurtured.

___ I usually find time to participate in hobbies and gatherings that I enjoy just for fun.

___ I have adequate social interactions outside of work or family.

___ I laugh easily, and experience plenty of joy in my life.

Total "I'm connecting" checks for section #5 ___

#6: Brain Training – *Cognitive Fitness*

We now take a look at your personal mental habits to see where you're already fit at cognitive levels and where you might want to improve.

Check any of the following that are true for you:

___ I seldom find myself multitasking.

___ I usually maintain sharp focus during the day.

___ I feel mentally challenged and stimulated on a regular basis.

___ I have recently learned a new skill (language, art, etc.) that challenged me and kept my mind sharp.

___ I actively seek out stimulating and challenging interactions and conversations with others.

___ I feel that I have a strong intent and sense of purpose in my life, which I connect with frequently during the day.

Total "I'm exercising my brain" checks for section #6 ___

Reflecting On & Interpreting Your Results

It's important to note that there are no good or bad scores for this assessment. I designed this tool to help you identify where to focus your time and energy to make the most significant changes as you start your training program.

If you find yourself running out of ink or needing to sharpen your pencil after making so many checkmarks, congratulations! On the other hand, if you didn't need to pick up your pen or pencil at all, don't panic. You are not alone. In fact, you're probably in the solid majority of people as they start this journey.

Although the concepts in this book are simple, it can be incredibly challenging to keep up with taking care of yourself in the midst of a very busy schedule.

The key to becoming *SHARP* is to take this process one small step at a time. Each new practice that you incorporate into your daily routine will make a big difference, and over time you will find yourself moving on to more advanced strategies that fully unleash the potential of your brain.

As we start to wrap up this chapter it's time to begin focusing on actions you can regularly take to wake up your full potential at work, and also make sure you have plenty of energy left after work for family and fun. As we'll be exploring throughout this book, how you breathe plays an essential role in how you perform, and stress constricts your natural breathing process.

Training Exercise #1: Breathing

The first step in breaking free from the effects of stress at work is to simply turn your attention to your breathing experience on a regular basis. As soon as you focus your attention on your breathing, your entire respiratory system begins almost instantly to self-correct and expand, bringing more oxygen to your brain.

Breathing exercises can be a wonderful way to start your day with focus and clarity, to recharge in the midst of a chaotic schedule, or to rebalance yourself physically, emotionally, mentally, and spiritually before transitioning home at the end of the day.

Focusing your attention to your breath might seem overly simplistic in the face of major stressors at work, but trust me, your ability to shift your attention temporarily away from stressing thoughts to the bodily experience of your inhales and exhales carries remarkable power to positively transform your brain performance.

At first you may find that watching your own breathing is in itself challenging. Most people do, because this seemingly simple shift from being lost in stressful thoughts to being focused on your inner experience is in reality a great leap of the mind.

Remember that any exercise is valuable only if, at first, it's a bit of a challenge to perform. So give yourself a few weeks to explore the power of 'breath recovery' in waking up energy and clarity.

Let's begin your actual training with a simple practice:

Even while reading these words, begin to focus your mind's attention more and more on the actual sensations you're experiencing in your nose ... in your chest ...
in your belly ... as you breathe.

Feel the air flowing in and out of your nose as the beginning point for the 'breath recovery' process ... don't make any effort to change your breathing, just feel it. The air flowing in ... the air flowing out ... and now expand your awareness to also include the sensations of movement in your chest and belly as you breathe.

Continue breathing freely for another minute or so ... and begin to notice how your breathing naturally, all on its own, begins to expand ... to deepen ... to become smoother ... and more enjoyable.

breathe ... and relax

For a 90-second guided meditation to help you focus on your breathing, scan the QR code below

CHAPTER 2
Boost Your Brainpower

We all know that we continue to change how we think and act throughout our lifespan. We live and learn, so the idea of having an adaptable brain would seem to be common knowledge. Yet until a few decades ago, the brain was thought to be hardwired from a very early age. Experts assumed that specific areas of the brain were responsible for specific functions, and that these could not be changed.

Although early research pioneers challenged this assumption, most people believed that the brain was pretty much 'set in stone' long before we reached adulthood. If you look at a traditional diagram of a brain, you'll see certain areas zoned for movement of particular parts of the body, certain areas for thinking, memory, judgment, hearing, and vision.

The medical assumption was that if you were to damage a particular area of your brain, you would lose the ability to perform that area's specified function. Case closed.

Well, not exactly. Over the past two decades, breakthrough studies have demonstrated that after a traumatic injury or a stroke, parts of the brain that were supposed to control one element of our functioning could actually be recruited to take over for another.

For example, individuals who became deaf after brain trauma began to show more activity in the area of the brain that controls visual function. Stroke victims who lost the ability to control one side of their body actually regained control and use of that disabled side, after the brain was given the time and stimulus to adapt.

New medical scanning technology (MRI) proved that brain function wasn't hardwired after all. Through a process formally called *neuroplasticity*, the brain somehow could reroute and rebuild itself, from the inside out.

A Simple Story of Brain Change

To see a video of author Heidi Hanna discussing how the brain adapts to training stimulation, scan the QR code below

Neuroplasticity refers to our brain's ability to be flexible, to change the shape and functioning of our system at neurological levels so that we can adapt to new challenges, learn new activities, and also heal ourselves when injured.

Even the word neuroplasticity itself is a bit daunting, not to mention all the scientific explanations of how the process functions at biochemical levels. In my work as a speaker and a coach, I've found that one of the best ways to explain a complex concept is to tell a story that helps to simplify it.

Imagine that you are the first to discover a new area of land, and you're faced with making your way through a giant field covered with all sorts of rugged gullies and overgrowth. I think of the thorn-covered blackberry fields I used to play around as a child, and how challenging it was to try to navigate through them when I wanted to pick berries or retrieve a foul ball from our wiffle ball game (and I still have the scars to prove it).

Now imagine that as a pioneer, you need to find your way across that treacherous field in search of much needed resources on the other side – perhaps fresh water, or wild boar for dinner, whatever it might be. The first time you try to clear your way, it's very challenging work. But eventually you push and plow across the rugged terrain, and discover that yes, the hard work of clearing the path was indeed worth it.

Next, imagine you have to repeat this same process over and over again, going across the field in order to get more resources. Most likely, rather than clearing a new path, you'll use the path you have already cleared (unless you discover a shortcut that might be even easier).

And as you continue following this path again and again, the path gets wider and clearer and you are able to get to your destination more quickly, using less energy along the way. Perhaps you've heard the saying, *"A journey of a thousand miles begins with a single step."* (Lao-tzu)

This is exactly how your brain was shaped as you were developing as a child. You were born with more than 100 billion brain cells (about 10 times the number of stars in the entire Milky Way and about 20 times the number of people on the planet) but relatively few established connections (or paths) linking them together.

When you were young, you were remarkably busy inside your own head, growing new connections and pathways very rapidly as your brain established a great many complex neurological patterns for movement, communication, thinking, etc. By age 3, your brain had navigated through fields in all directions and formed about 1,000 trillion connections. That number is about twice as many connections as grown adults have. Why? Because as you entered into adolescence, your brain naturally began a process of neural "pruning" in order to eliminate unnecessary connections.

What's the inherent wisdom in this pruning of unneeded or duplicate pathways? It takes energy to maintain these connections – so you don't want to have to keep landscaping ten different paths through your territory when one will do you fine.

The human organism is designed to run as an efficient machine, and so during adolescence it step-by-step shuts down and stops maintaining duplicate or unneeded neural pathways. As we grow older, part of the aging process includes a lessening of our ability to create and maintain new pathways in the brain. However, we do continue to have the capacity to both establish new pathways and strengthen those that exist at any age.

What's more, we also have the ability to use more effective mental tools as we get older, to help clear neural paths quicker and more effectively. These tools are exactly what will be described later in this book.

This story of clearing paths and making them easier for us to navigate is a very simplified metaphor for how we create new ways of thinking, establish new habits, and even change behaviors. When we don't use established pathways for a while, they tend to become inefficient and overgrown; it's harder to perform certain mental activities, for instance. But when those pathways are used regularly through cognitive exercise, our minds stay sharp.

Certainly it's more difficult to 'teach an old dog new tricks,' because we lose much of our early childhood mental flexibility as we grow older. But by employing high power cognitive tools for learning, we can continue to develop our brains actively in directions that serve us.

The Exercise Factor: Medical Proof

You know exercise is good for you. You experience from the inside out that it makes you smarter, happier, and healthier.

As Harvard professor John Ratey describes in his groundbreaking book *Spark: The Revolutionary New Science of Exercise and the Brain*, regular aerobic exercise has been proven to stimulate a chemical called BDNF (*brain-derived neurotrophic factor*) that acts like 'Miracle-Gro' to brain cells.[1]

Within this scientific model, it's been shown that when you consistently challenge your brain, you strengthen neurological pathways, making it easier for you to think and act in the ways that you want to.

This structural support system, known as myelin sheath, is a fatty tissue that makes connections between brain cells more effective and efficient. And because it is live tissue, it must be regularly maintained with nutrients and activity, just like any other part of your body.

You have to use it, or you lose it.

If you stop repeating a particular neurological pathway in your brain, it will start to become more challenging to navigate; and after considerable time off, you'll have to make a new effort to break through the 'overgrowth' and re-establish a fluent flow. This is why it's crucial to regularly exercise those aspects of your thinking mind that you want to keep sharp!

The strategies discussed in the next few chapters will present cognitive tools that will enable you to clear and maintain solid connections between all of the brain cells that need to communicate effectively with each other, in order for you to think and behave in ways that support your most important personal and professional goals.

Beyond Survival Mode

Just like the rest of our body, the brain works in a way optimally suited for our biological survival. Because we require constant energy to fuel our cells, and because our natural energy supply is limited, our control center is designed to expend as little energy as possible. We also are genetically preprogrammed to want to accumulate stores of energy (calories from food) in reserve for when we might run out. Especially when physical survival might be threatened, the more we have and the less we need, the better off we should be.

This made perfect sense in times gone by; the problem today is that our ancient automatic-pilot mode, designed to help us survive in more primitive settings, is actually counter-productive to maintaining a healthy lifestyle.

According to cognitive scientists, we have two unique processing systems in the brain that are always vying for dominance: the ancient automated system (or auto-brain), and the newer reflective system (or thinking brain).

In times of danger, the automated system takes over and allows us to act quickly, which is important when we need to react to a threat or run away from danger. "Don't think, just do."

When faced with choices requiring reflection, the thinking mind takes over, using whatever time is needed to make the best decision for the situation. Learning, judgment, evaluating, and emotional responses are all part of the reflective system.

For raw survival purposes, our auto-brain has to be ready to take charge at any moment. Even in contemporary times, there are sudden dangerous occasions when taking time to think through or debate multiple choices could leave us dead in our tracks, such as a truck barreling right at us on the road, or a fire rapidly burning in our home. Times like these call for an immediate response, a preprogrammed knee-jerk reaction to a situation.

The automated function of the mind predates the thinking function by many millions of years. In fact, it's often called mammalian or 'monkey brain' to differentiate it from the newly evolved rational section of the human brain capable of complex analytical thought.

And to complete the neurological picture, we also have in our head what's called the reptilian 'lizard brain,' which we share with almost all other animals on the planet.

In sum:

- Deep down at the base of the human brain in the cerebellum and brainstem, the reptilian 'lizard brain' controls our most basic instincts and regulates all of our automatic unconscious bodily functions.

- One step up, our 'monkey brain' controls our more complex functions related to emotional reactions. Most mammals lead with their 'monkey brain,' which fuels the basic responses to fear and desire.

- The cognitive thinking 'human brain' consists of the outer layer of brain tissue surrounding the 'monkey brain,' specifically what are called the forebrain and the frontal lobes. This cognitive area allows for logical, emotionless thought, such as deductive reasoning and delayed gratification.

By using our unique human brain, we are able to think through and determine our responses to a situation rather than just reacting. When we are faced with sudden threats to our system, we often don't have time to stop and analyze what's going on. During these times we are glad to have our 'lizard' and 'monkey' brains to quickly get us to safety, employing our reflexive fight-or-flight response.

But usually, we do best when we consciously observe our habitual 'monkey' and 'lizard' reactions to situations; and when those reactions are not to our advantage, learn how to change our programming.

Here's the key point of this chapter: Through purposeful cognitive training, we can take conscious steps to modify our automated programming, and thus change our lives for the better!

Avoid Multitasking Disasters

One of the key insights to come recently from cognitive science is that when we multitask, we tend to drop out of high level rational decision making, and slip into 'monkey brain' reactions in our various split activities.

Because we have so many things going on at one time when we multitask, we operate mostly on automatic pilot, rather than reflecting upon our decisions and actions.

Multitasking often provokes mindless decisions that may end up causing serious problems with important responsibilities or relationships. Next time you find yourself trying to do a million things at once and getting irritable or grumpy with someone you care about, remind yourself that you're using your 'monkey brain,' and work on acting more like a rational human being - giving each moment your full attention, so that you respond in a more thoughtful, beneficial way.

You may also consider trying something I've done with a few close friends: When someone seems distracted, ask them if they're using their 'monkey brain' (use this method at your own risk).

"My employer is paying for the surgery. I'm having a speed bump installed between my brain and my mouth."

Not Just Creatures of Habit

There are two reasons why this single-focus concept is critical to our brain training program:

First, we need to keep in mind that many of our judgments, decisions, and actions do not emerge from a place of thoughtful consideration or mindfulness.

Too often we are creatures of habit. We react to a situation or a person based on previous prejudice and programming, or our 'lizard brain' fight or flight reflexes, rather than relating consciously using whole-brain intelligence and wisdom.

Second, and most important, when our past programming is less than desirable, we possess the inner ability to train our auto-brain to respond differently.

In the spirit of neuroplasticity, we can repeatedly aim our focused attention in particular directions that stimulate the creation of new pathways, or the expansion of old ones, so that we learn new and improved mental and behavioral patterns.

There are many examples of this core re-training process in sports and other types of competition. Skilled chess players and elite athletes have trained themselves to analyze complex situations more quickly in order to respond in the best way, as fast as possible. Through practice, these superstars are able to consciously train elements of their brain that normally would be part of the reflective, thoughtful system to happen automatically, without much time or energy.

In Praise Of The Auto-Brain

There are loads of examples of the auto-brain in action throughout one's daily routines. Think of all of the things you do during the day that you could almost do in your sleep (and maybe sometimes you do). You get up and turn the coffee pot on, brush your teeth, take a shower, get dressed, drive to work, walk to your office. Did you really have to pay much attention to get all those things done?

Because our auto-brain requires a very small amount of energy compared to rational decision making, it's always going to be the preferred way of perceiving a situation, processing information, and facilitating behavior.

Our auto-brain is certainly not a bad thing. It's actually a most marvelous phenomenon, as long as we remain aware of how it functions, so that we can be sure it's moving us in the right direction.

Your ongoing conscious awareness in the present moment is key to making sure your automated functions and reflex habits are actually serving you, not deterring you.

Even when we're not very conscious of what's happening around us, our brain assesses situations constantly, making associative and habitual interpretations that are often accurate. And the auto-brain tends to see what it expects to.

Here is a good example of how your auto-brain works. Read through this paragraph and see how much you understand:

> "According to a research study at Cmabridge University, it deosn't mttaer in what order the ltteers in a word are, the only iprmoetnt thing is that the frist and lsat ltteer be in the rghit pclae. The rset can be a total mses and you can still raed it wouthit porbelms. Tish is bcuseae the human mind does not raed ervey lteter by istlef, but the word as a wlohe."

People are often surprised by how easily they can read the paragraph above. Because our brain focuses primarily on patterns and is able to make assumptions, even gibberish can make sense as long as certain patterns remain consistent (which, in this case, means the first and last letters are accurate).

Remember, your brain wants to conserve energy for potential threats during the day, so as often as possible, it prefers automatic pilot mode. Habits save us a great amount of mental energy. In *The Power of Full Engagement*, co-author Jim Loehr, one of my mentors, proposes that **up to 95% of human behavior happens in this automated state of mind, while only about 5% is conscious, self-regulated behavior.**[2]

We call these automated activities our habits; they enable us to get much more done during the day than would be possible if we had to concentrate our full conscious attention on tying our shoes and brushing our teeth. Habits are patterns of thought and behavior that have been performed so often and served us so well that they become programmed into our auto-brains and no longer require our full attention.

Changing Pathways – Improving Habits

The development of new habits is one of the primary survival strategies of living organisms. But we can become conditioned with bad habits (ones that undermine a healthy, fulfilling life) just as easily as the good ones. And those stubborn bad habits are very difficult to change, because they happen automatically after years of our training them to do so, whether we were trying intentionally or not.

Everything we think or do in life, whether positive or negative, has a training effect – and if done often enough, establishes a new habitual pattern.

This means that if you find yourself grabbing fast food on a regular basis, you will soon feel pulled in that direction when you start to get hungry. Stay up late several nights working (or writing a book), and you will train your brain to see this as the norm, making falling asleep at a decent hour much more challenging. If you sit at your desk too much and don't get up and go outside for regular exercise, you're reinforcing yet another unhealthy habit.

Repetition is the primary act of training. Anything you do often enough becomes a habit. For instance, if you fixate on negative worried thinking, you're going to develop a mental habit and may find yourself stuck thinking about what's bad in life instead of noticing what's good.

And once you have a bad habit, unless you consciously make an effort to change it, your brain will keep these pathways 'well-paved' as you automatically continue using them. The brain training principles discussed in the next chapters will show you how to consciously change the focus of your mental energy, so as to develop more supportive habits that are less draining, and thus easier to maintain.

With such an amazing operating system that can help us automate important processes in our lives, we can choose to actively train our brains to move us regularly in the right direction – and thus make our auto-brains truly serve us.

Pay Attention

In this light, note that your power to change habits depends on your choice of where you focus your attention, each moment of the day. In fact, your habits of attention can be seen as the bedrock of all your habits. Notice that most of the time during the day, you aren't taking conscious control of where you focus your attention, it's operating on automatic pilot.

Only when you start taking more responsibility for where you focus your mental energy, do you become fully in control of your life.

Any and all cognitive training requires that you consciously decide to focus your attention in particular directions that serve you well – that's what cognitive training is all about. You shift your attention in a new or valued direction, and continue to hold your focus in that direction while you perform certain mental actions, or while you observe certain natural happenings, such as your breathing.

And in this process of disciplined focused attention, over time and repetition you develop a new habit designed specifically to improve your life.

Training Exercise #2:
Shifting Into 'Zero-Task' Mode

To further this conscious habit-building theme, let's end this chapter by continuing with the mental focusing exercise already introduced – that of pausing and refocusing your attention to your breathing habits. We will expand that cognitive-shifting experience a step, so that you quickly let go of multitasking and other mental stressors, and start reinforcing new habits that bring more oxygen to your brain, while also de-conditioning old thought patterns and breathing habits that don't serve you.

As we did before, while you continue reading, begin this exercise by 'doing' nothing at all, except refocusing your mind's attention gently toward the sensation that's happening all the time inside your own nose. Just tune into sensory mode here in this moment, where your breath reflex is continuing to bring oxygen into your lungs and ultimately to your brain, and then blowing the used-up air (carbon dioxide) out through your nose (or mouth).

Notice that, at first, your breathing is still operating mostly on automatic pilot. Probably for the last hour at least, you've been mostly unconscious of your breathing experience, even though how you're breathing is so important to your overall vitality and performance.

As you focus your conscious attention on your body's breathing patterns, simply be the observer, and notice how your breathing quite quickly begins to change for the better (deeper and more relaxed) when you pay attention to it.

Here we find a key to behavior change: when you focus your attention on a habit, you can directly perceive its effect on your body and wellbeing, and that very act of perceiving the effect will stimulate needed change.

For instance, right now as you continue experiencing the sensations happening because of your breathing – both in your nose and also in your chest and belly – if and when tensions begin to relax, and as you become more relaxed, notice that you feel better. This direct perception is a powerful teacher. And you can trust this teacher to guide your focus in rewarding directions.

If you find your attention wandering away from your breathing, back to thinking about this and that, here's an addition to the exercise that will bring your attention 100% into the present moment, free of all multitasking temptations.

As you continue watching your breaths come and go, with every inhale and exhale, repeat the following words:

(exhale ...) Relax...
(inhale ...) Renew

or for a variation, try the following phrase:

(exhale ...) I
(inhale ...) am
(exhale ...) here
(inhale ...) now
(exhale ...) breathing
(inhale ...) freely

Making no effort to breathe in any particular way, repeat the words "relax, renew" or move four times through this 3-breath cycle of the words, "I am here now breathing freely". Notice whatever cognitive-shift experience happens within you, caused by just one minute of focusing entirely on words and sensations that aim your attention on mind-body presence in the here and now.

breathe ... and experience the present

CHAPTER 3
The *SHARP* Brain Recharge Process

In order to be *SHARP*, it's important that we train our brain strategically so that we can bring our best mental energy, focus, and attention to the people and things that matter most to us. But unfortunately, most of us tend to run ourselves into the ground with non-stop, high-speed, stressful mental activity during the day.

- We multitask, which causes stress

- We worry a lot, which takes loads of energy out of our available inner supply

- We work against deadlines, which cause chronic anxiety

- We stay in problem-solving gear without a break for too long, which strains our system

- We get stuck in shallow tense breathing, which reduces the flow of oxygen to our brain

- We remain sitting for far too long, which further stresses our body and zaps our vitality

You can learn to develop a periodic 'recharge' process to use several times during the day – a new habit that will almost instantly shift you out of stress-fatigue mode, into recovery-recharge mode.

In this chapter I will teach you a short and enjoyable recovery process where you spend just three minutes, three times a day turning your thinking brain off, to just relax, rebalance, and recharge.

Scheduling firm appointments to recharge your energy and sharpness needs to be a priority every day!

I'll say it again, your energy is not an unlimited resource; therefore, taking care of yourself is not an option. It's a necessity! You must invest in yourself regularly if you want to have anything to give to others.

By investing strategically in our own energy management, we create a win-win-win for our self, our family, and our career.

To see a video of author Heidi Hanna talking about the SHARP Brain Recharge, scan the QR code below

Reasons to Recharge

Your brain is a remarkable system that can perceive outside sensations, process that data, and respond physically, emotionally, and intellectually. The brain can consider and reflect upon a situation based on memory association, then generate ideas and orchestrate game plans to accomplish your goals.

Meanwhile, at mostly unconscious levels, the brain is running your entire physiological show from heartbeat to saline balance to muscular performance and the rest – and this all takes energy!

Specifically with the brain and stress-versus-performance, you are designed to spend a portion of your mental energy:

- thinking and problem-solving
- perceiving and enjoying your bodily experience
- feeling emotions and relating
- focusing inward toward relaxation and peace

When it comes to the performance and health of your brain, balance is what's best, and in the long-term required. However, most of us have developed long held habits of fixating too much on the first function in that four part list you just read.

Think back to being in the classroom – just like being in the board room – forced for long periods of time each day to sit still in one immobile position, and focus solely on thinking, as opposed to perceiving, feeling, and enjoying movement and relaxation. This is the story of mankind for the last hundred years or so, and our habits are deeply ingrained.

My premise in this book is that we must regain a healthy balance between the four primary natural functions of the human brain if we're to feel better, be healthier, and have higher mental levels of performance.

We all know what it feels like to be burnt out. We reach that point all too often where we've temporarily exhausted our biochemical supplies of brain food and brain hormones, and just can't think straight or relate well at all.

What's the solution? We need to dedicate time where we strategically shift our focus away from stress producing mental activities toward rejuvenation activities.

This can be done quickly, and if practiced regularly (at least three times a day), it will bring remarkable uplifts of vitality, clarity, empathy, and creativity; four of the boosts we need most in order to be successful and to enjoy life at work and at home.

The *SHARP* Recharge process has three key intentions:

1. Recover: In general, most of us do not need to do more, we need to do less. On average we're over-stressed, not under-stressed. This means that a crucial item for our daily to-do list is to periodically and intentionally not do anything at all. Perhaps this idea seems to run contrary to the whole notion of training the brain to perform at higher levels, but just the opposite is true.

We all realize that physically we can't expect to run non-stop. We must take breather breaks, and discipline ourselves to pause, rest, and recover. The idea is not to train harder, but to train smarter.

To be stronger we need to create a stimulus that causes us to adapt. However, when it comes to working out our brain, most people are overtraining, which leads to all sorts of overuse injuries that not only slow us down, but literally wear down the structure of the brain.

When we are able to get mental recovery on a regular basis, we reduce the symptoms of overuse, and keep our operating system strong.

2. Rebalance. When we pause to get back in tune with our natural breathing process and stimulate the relaxation response in the body and the brain, our system can regain its natural state of internal balance, or homeostasis. Studies consistently show that when we are out of balance, we experience chronic stress, worry, confusion, and fatigue, because our brain is unable to operate efficiently.

Regularly choosing to regain balance by shifting our attention away from mental and emotional stressors toward positive, present moment physical experience enables our mind to return to a more harmonious state. This allows us to be more collaborative, creative, and hopeful.

When our brain is in a positive, balanced state, we can perform at our best and keep our operating system flexible.

3. Recharge. As mentioned before, our mental energy is not a limitless resource. In order to keep our system functioning at its best over time, we must strategically invest energy back into it. We do this primarily by refocusing our attention temporarily away from all of the energy-draining, problem-solving thinking toward the primary charging mechanism of our body, our breathing.

You have already begun to experiment with this recharge process. Every time you tune into your breath experience you show yourself love and support because, as you've already begun to notice, once you shift your focus to your breathing, your mind temporarily lets go of the habitual fixations that often drain you.

Instead, you focus on the oxygen intake system that directly brings new energy into your brain and body. When your breathing is tense, shallow, and constantly stopping on the inhale or the exhale, your entire being is caught up in that tension and the natural flow is compromised.

You must consciously act regularly to break this stressed-breathing habit. This is a primary brain-training challenge, and you will need to commit seriously to the Brain Recharge practice in order to create a new positive 'free breath' habit.

The focus statements you learned at the end of the last chapter, "Relax, renew" and "I am here now, breathing freely" are core intentions that you can hold in the back of your mind during the day to focus on, especially during the 3-minute recharge breaks.

By scheduling this specific recovery time throughout the day, you will increase your energy holistically – physically, mentally, emotionally, and spiritually – so that you're running on a full tank and able to be your best self. A brain that is full of energy is one that supports your health, happiness, and performance, keeping your operating system functioning optimally over time for maximum endurance.

I realize that asking anyone to spend 9 minutes a day focusing on something other than work is a lot to ask. However, you are your most valuable resource. If you don't take care of yourself, you can't possibly take care of anyone or anything else. (Are you starting to get my point here?)

Just ... Pause & Relax

Meditation has become a buzzword for relaxation programs because many quality studies have shown that meditation can quiet the mind and calm the body. But most people struggle with a meditation practice because they lack the structure or guidelines necessary to begin, or because they're trying to learn a challenging process too quickly.

Traditional meditation has been portrayed in the media as being something for only gurus and their followers. Indeed some forms of meditation are quite difficult to master and require a teacher. But new approaches to what is called 'short-form meditation' take only 3-5 minutes a session, can be learned readily, and can be included in a busy workday as a vital lifeline to refreshing mental energy and focusing attention.

Anyone can use this short-form type of meditation quite easily as a tool once they understand the key principles.

A Recharge Break is all about refocusing your attention in rewarding directions. In order for such a focusing meditation to be effective, it should include the following:

- A time-frame set aside for the recharge experience (scheduled as a priority)
- A comfortable position (whatever feels relaxing to you)
- A somewhat quiet environment (free from distractions)
- A mental focusing device or technique (sound or word that is repeated)
- A non-judgmental attitude (not critical of yourself or your process)

61

Of course, there will be times when you can't escape to your 'man cave' to meditate, but this is no reason not to take a recharge break. Don't let your environment dictate your life.

Regardless of your surroundings, you can always just close your eyes, or look at something calming in your office. Focus your attention toward your inner experience of breathing and whole-body presence, and perhaps bring to mind a focus phrase that will quickly shift your brain into a sensory experience that stimulates your natural sense of balance and well-being.

What we're considering in this chapter is that you can use discipline to initiate the relaxing, not just flexing, of your mental muscles. Consciously focusing on your breathing initiates a return to a smoother, more relaxed breathing process.

At work, you can take your breath awareness with you after a Recharge Break, so that you continue to reap the benefits in the midst of a hectic routine.

Recharge Tools and Strategies

It's often difficult to get a busy brain to take a break from stressful fixations. The basic process you're learning in this book will help greatly, and you might also benefit from using tools such as audio tracks or meditation videos designed to help you effortlessly re-focus your attention and minimize distracting thoughts.

I encourage you to go to my website and explore the excellent multi-media meditation tools that are available. My colleagues and I have developed a number of guided experiences that will help you considerably both in developing new recharge habits and regularly moving through them.

As you come to realize that you do have a certain amount of control and freedom to maintain a calmer state of mind at work and at home, you may want to consider additional ways to provide environmental support for yourself; such as soft or inspirational music, beautiful photographs of calming places or friends and family, light dimmers, a desk-top waterfall, or aromatherapy.

When you're home, you'll find that just lighting a candle or heating up some scented oil in a burner can instantly help bring you into a more calm state of mind.

To visit the SHARP Brain Gym, go to
http://www.synergyprograms.com/braingym
or scan the QR code below

The Full *SHARP* Brain Recharge Process

You've already been introduced to the general framework of the *SHARP* Brain Recharge Process in earlier chapters, and hopefully right now you're continuing to stay aware of your breathing, even while reading these words.

Like any good habit, the more you do it, the better it makes you feel and perform – so the more ingrained it becomes.

However, here in the beginning, don't be surprised if just turning your attention to your breathing seems like a real challenge. That's why I'm here as your coach, to help you with the initial steps of developing a new brain fitness routine, so that you make it successfully through the habit-formation process.

Let's look a little more closely at the five dimensions of a successful Recharge Break that I listed earlier in this chapter, so that you have a solid sense of how to approach your new habit:

1. Scheduling: A habit is something that you repeat fairly regularly. You will need to discipline yourself to do this exercise three times a day if possible. This means making an effort to set aside the time and sticking with your intention. If you don't do this, you simply will not train the new habit, and you won't experience any gain.

So right now, see if you're willing to dedicate 9 minutes a day to a brain training exercise of great value. If so, take a few minutes to plug in a Recharge Break 3 times a day for the next week to get started. I'd highly recommend setting an alarm to remind you and hopefully to help snap you out of work mode.

I encourage you to commit to one month of doing this self-discipline process. At the end of the month you can evaluate the results, examine the new habit, and decide if you want to sustain it long-term.

2. Quiet Environment: When you're home, it's relatively easy to retreat into a quiet room on a consistent basis, establish a regular place to sit or lie down, and move through the Recharge Break. But when you're at work, you'll just have to make do with your situation as best you can.

What's important is not to be overly fussy about a perfect environment when you take your break. Discipline yourself to take a break and move through the 3-minute process regardless of where you are so that you can train yourself to recharge in any circumstance.

You might want to consider explaining to your employer and fellow workers what you're doing during your 3-minute breaks, so that you get their understanding and support. Ideally your employer will make Recharge Breaks company policy on a voluntary basis, because everyone gains when you pause and refresh!

3. Comfortable Posture: It is not necessary to sit in the traditional 'full lotus' cross-legged position in order to achieve the benefits of meditation. Sitting upright in your chair at work will do fine.

What's important here is that you settle into a comfortable posture, ideally with an upright spine, so that your body feels aligned and balanced.

As you focus on your breathing in this position, give yourself a few moments to move around and adjust. Don't force yourself to sit still at first. Let that stillness happen organically as you start to settle down.

Your breathing will naturally move your body a bit. After all, breathing is movement. Sit more upright as you inhale, even resettling in your chair, and then contract your belly muscles and let your chin drop as you exhale completely.

4. Mental Focusing Aid or Technique: Traditional meditation often asks you to watch your breaths coming and going for half an hour – and that's it, you're on your own. But this is very hard to do for most of us because our thoughts immediately spring back into rapid shifting work-mode, and we lose the vital awareness of our breathing and whole-body presence.

This is where the traditional 'mantra' or short repeated saying lends a helpful hand, and new cognitive insights have enabled us to develop statements and other refocusing techniques that greatly enhance the recharge process.

For instance, you've already learned to use the words "Renew, relax" and the focus statement "I am here, now, breathing freely." If either of these works for you, continue with it, because it is very powerful to bring your attention to the present moment, to your breathing, and to the intent of letting go as you set your breathing free to return to its natural rhythm and flow.

Your Own Focus Statement: Within this process of mental shifting, there are some classic phrases that have been shown to be effective, but you're always free to come up with your own variations to make the experience more personalized and meaningful to you. Often the process of inventing your own focus statement enables you to discover a special 'mantra' that is ideally suited for you, so feel free to experiment.

For the Recharge Break, you'll want to use a focus statement that aims your attention in the here and now, focuses toward sensations rather than thoughts or memories, and encourages relaxation rather than stress.

Examples of focus phrases include:

"Be here, now"	"One"
"Clear and present"	"Calm"
"I feel light and energized"	"Recharging"
"I am investing in myself"	"I am renewed"

Visual Aids for Focusing: Many people benefit from keeping their eyes open rather than closed, and looking at a beautiful picture of nature or piece of artwork that focuses their attention calmly.

Just be sure you don't look at a picture that is filled with emotional associations because that can lead you off into memories and imaginations that take you away from the rejuvenation of the present moment.

Audio Aids for Focusing: Quiet, non-emotional music can help in the relaxation and centering process, as long as it stays in the background and doesn't carry you away from your focus on your breathing. Likewise, guided audio sessions can be valuable if they're not too complex.

As you begin to train your brain to focus in the moment, an audio aid can help you resist the natural tendency to shift to future and past experiences. With practice, you may find any noise to be somewhat distracting, and prefer to quiet your mind without any external guidance. Stay tuned into your process each time you recharge, and you'll begin to discover your own best practices.

Breath Counting: This is a very good beginning point for creating mental stillness and refreshing your brain. As you stay fully aware of all the breath sensations and movements, count each exhale one after the other and become naturally quiet in your mind on the inhale.

This counting combined with focusing on your breathing will almost immediately quiet the flow of thoughts through the mind, which is the shortest route to instant rejuvenation.

5. Non-judgmental Attitude: A key to success with this type of mental exercise is to put aside all evaluation or judgment of how you're doing with the process. There is no right or wrong here, no good or bad performance. In fact, this is not about performance at all, but about shifting from one mental mode (thinking) to another mental mode (experiencing) quickly and completely.

Cognitive studies have proven that most stress is caused by chronic judgmental or worried thoughts that habitually dominate your mind. When you shift your attention to present-moment bodily sensations, all thoughts temporarily cease, and you experience relief.

In the same way that you can't make an effort to relax a physical muscle, you can't make an effort to relax your mind. You must simply choose to let go and focus attention onto an effortless, natural bodily function such as your breathing. Then you are free to enjoy the temporary peace and quiet when all thoughts stop.

Training Exercise #3:
The Expanded Brain Recharge Process

Each time you pause for three minutes, begin by sitting quietly in a calm environment. For a few moments, just gently turn your attention to your breath experience in your nose, your chest, and your belly. Let your body move as you settle into the recharge session. Once you feel fully focused on your breathing and your experience in the present moment, you can either:

a) *continue with your basic breath watch for a couple more minutes, with each breath bringing new energy into your system,*

b) *say a focus phrase to yourself several times, such as "I am here, now, breathing freely," or whatever statement you choose,*

c) *focus on a picture or object as you stay fully aware of your breathing at the same time,*

d) *watch or listen to a video or audio recording that guides you through a simple meditation,*

e) *count your breaths to hold your attention on your breathing and quiet any thoughts.*

The aim is to open up free time and space within you, without any thinking stress, so that with each new breath you recharge your system with new energy, hope, enjoyment, and balance.

breathe ... relax ... recharge

PART TWO

Brain Health Fundamentals

SYNERGY Fab 5

*"To keep the body in good health is a duty ...
otherwise we shall not be able to keep
our mind strong and clear."*

Buddha, circa 500 BC

Before we look specifically at how to improve cognitive fitness, we need to explore the key lifestyle behaviors that determine general physical, emotional, and mental fitness. Optimizing these elements will prove critical in making sure that the cognitive training you engage in is effective.

In a sense, it's like using the right materials to make certain that the work you do will take hold and last over time – building a solid foundation. Each component helps your body to create the right brain chemistry to help neurons communicate most effectively and stay strong and resilient over time.

To tackle each of the elements that are within our control, I have created the *SYNERGY* Fab 5. They are valuable guidelines to follow when your goal is optimal health, happiness, and performance of the body and mind. Each component has a synergistic effect when combined with the others:

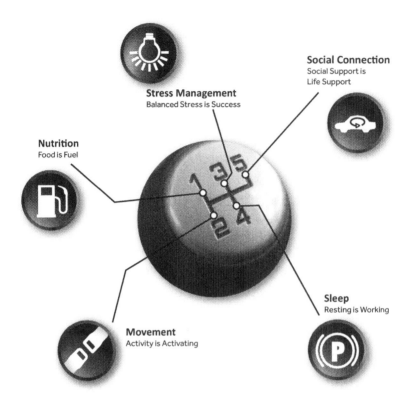

1. Nutrition – Food is Fuel

2. Physical Movement – Activity is Activating

3. Stress Management – Balancing Stress Balances Life

4. Sleep – Resting is Working

5. Connection – Social Support is Life Support

In the next five chapters, we'll look at each of these in more depth.

CHAPTER 4
Nutrition – Food is Fuel

"Let food be thy medicine." – Hippocrates

How we choose to fuel our body might be the most important choice we make when it comes to our brainpower. The glucose we get from the foods we eat is the primary source of fuel for our brain.

Though the brain takes up only about 2% of total body mass, it utilizes approximately 20% of the glucose and oxygen we consume.

In order to keep this energy-demanding organ functioning at its best, it is critical that we keep glucose levels steady throughout the day, and that we boost our brain health with foods that enhance and nourish both the structure and function of our brain.

There are three key strategies to optimizing nutrition for brain health:

- First, eat small amounts regularly throughout the day
- Second, eat in a way that balances your blood sugar at each meal and snack
- And third, maximize the brain-building benefits of eating by choosing high-nutrient 'power foods'

Keep in mind, these are the same strategies I would recommend if this book were about feeling more energetic, enhancing performance in physical training or an athletic event, improving heart health, decreasing the risk of developing diabetes, or managing weight.

The fundamentals are always the same, and they are the most important strategies to focus on as you develop your *SHARP* nutrition plan.

Following these simple guidelines will get you far in your journey towards health and performance goals, whatever they may be. In fact, I'd say the fundamentals make up at least 85–90% of the equation, no matter what you're trying to improve.

You will notice that I'm calling these suggestions "strategies," and this is intentional. They are goals that you want to strive for, but not that you're expected to do 100% of the time.

In order to have a sustainable nutrition plan, it's important to avoid making it overly rigid. Otherwise, your tendency will be to rebel against the rules or follow an all-or-nothing mentality of being either "on" or "off" a diet. If you are able to use these strategies regularly, you won't feel guilty for an occasional indulgence.

The recommendations below are simple to grasp, but not necessarily easy to implement due to the way we've trained ourselves to use food in the past. In the first part of this section, we will cover what you should be doing with your nutrition plan for optimal brain health. Second, we will talk about why these simple strategies are so important and the overall impact they will have on your brain and your body.

Finally, I will discuss important ways that you can use your brain to improve your diet, while you use your diet to improve your brain.

Key Strategy #1 – Eat Light and Often

In order to keep glucose levels consistent and avoid dipping into 'survival mode' throughout the day, it is critical to eat in a way that keeps you in your optimal blood sugar (glucose) range. A lack of glucose starves the brain of energy, while too much can cause system overload. In fact, science shows that insulin spikes may be quite damaging to brain cells, which could be why some brain experts consider Alzheimer's disease to be "Type 3 diabetes."[1]

While there is no exact ideal blood glucose level or one-size-fits-all approach to accomplishing this optimal state, a good rule of thumb is to eat something that causes you to feel satisfied but not full, approximately every 3–4 hours during the day.

Determining what this eating plan looks like can be challenging. In *The Blue Zones*, author Dan Buettner describes how the Okinawan people follow a philosophy of eating in moderation called "hari hachi bu," or eating to the point you feel 80% full.[2]

Because it can take up to 20 minutes for your brain to recognize satiety signals from the body, and because we tend to eat so darn fast these days, aiming for 80% can be a useful strategy to end up on target. For most people, this equates to about 4 handfuls of food at meals (1 handful of carbohydrates, 1 handful of protein, and 2 handfuls of fruits and vegetables), and about 100–150 calories at each snack.

Key Strategy #2 – Eat Balanced Meals

To make sure our glucose levels aren't spiking or crashing, it's also important to have the right combination of nutrients:

complex carbohydrates, lean protein, and healthy fat. For an ideal brain-healthy plate, I recommend a **25/25/50** split of foods (carbohydrate/ protein/fruits and vegetables) to keep blood sugar levels balanced and maximize the amount of "power foods" you get in your meal, primarily from produce filled with brain-protecting nutrients.

It is important to have a variety of energy sources at each meal: quick energy providers in carbohydrates and slower sources of energy in fat and protein.

As living plant sources, fruits and vegetables develop protective phytochemicals called antioxidants to help them avoid environmental damage. Upon consumption, these nutrients can also help protect our body and brain from damage that occurs as a byproduct of our normal metabolic process.

Key Strategy #3 – Eat Foods With High Nutritional Value

For optimal brain health, focus on maximizing the number of beneficial foods that you eat (natural, fresh, unprocessed) and minimizing those that may be harmful (fried or processed foods, fatty meat and dairy).

A recent report by the National Institutes of Health stated that among all of the evidence reviewed, only two strategies were shown to have good support for their ability to decrease the development of Alzheimer's and dementia: cognitive training (which we will discuss in part three of this book) and a Mediterranean diet.[3]

The Mediterranean diet (based on commonly consumed cuisine in areas of the Mediterranean, such as Spain, Italy, and Greece) includes fresh foods that offer a balance of nutrients, including whole-grain carbohydrates, lean protein, fruits and vegetables, and healthy fat. Eating such foods stabilizes blood glucose, providing a consistent and stable source of fuel for the body and brain.

The quality of nutrients in these foods also has a high impact. You get lots of monounsaturated fat, omega-3 fat, lean protein, fiber, and many vitamins, minerals, and other protective nutrients such as antioxidants and polyphenols. At the same time, the Mediterranean diet decreases the focus on foods that may be harmful to our health, such as saturated fat, trans fat, and highly processed carbohydrates.

In a study of two thousand Manhattan residents averaging 76 years of age, those eating a Mediterranean diet had a 68 percent lower risk of developing Alzheimer's disease.[4]

To see a video of author Heidi Hanna talking about nutrition
for brain health and optimal performance,
scan the QR code below

Power Foods

Below you will find a list that will help boost your brain health and performance. Aim for a plant-based, Mediterranean diet that focuses on the list below, and minimize eating food that may be damaging, including processed foods, saturated and trans fats, alcohol in excess, and added sugar.

- Fish (or fish oil supplements)
- Poultry and other lean meats
- Beans and legumes
- Eggs (including yolks)
- Low fat milk, cheese, and yogurt
- Nuts and seeds: almonds, cashews, walnuts, hazelnuts, Brazil nuts, peanuts, sunflower seeds, sesame seeds, flax seed, peanut butter, almond butter
- Olives, olive oil, avocado
- Whole grains

- Fruits (especially berries) and dark colored fruit juices (such as Concord grape and pomegranate)
- Vegetables (especially leafy greens like spinach and lettuces, red bell peppers, broccoli, and broccoli sprouts)
- Wine (in moderation)
- Coffee and tea (in moderation)
- Spices, especially turmeric, ginger, cinnamon, saffron, and garlic

Power foods will make your brain work better by offering key building blocks that strengthen its structure. (For more information on how specific nutrients impact brain health and function, see *The SHARP Diet.*)

What's Good for the Heart is Good for the Brain

Because circulation of glucose and oxygen is critical to keep the brain fueled appropriately, it is important to make sure that you eat in a way that is optimal for blood flow. This means keeping arteries clear from excess cholesterol, triglycerides, and inflammation. What is good for the heart is good for the brain.

A Mediterranean diet consisting of lean protein, whole grains, and healthy fat will promote heart health. That means you'll help your heart and your brain by eating in a way that keeps unhealthy cholesterol at bay and decreases inflammation.

The tools: healthy fats found in foods like nuts, seeds, and olive oil, omega-3 fatty acids in fish, fiber in beans and lentils, and antioxidants and other phytochemicals in fruits, vegetables, wine, coffee, tea, and spices.

To keep triglycerides in a healthy range, it is important to limit or avoid processed carbohydrates (such as white bread, white rice, crackers, pretzels, and chips) and added sugars, and to keep alcohol consumption to a moderate amount (1-2 servings a day).

Maintain a Healthy Weight

Many neuroscientists suggest that a healthy weight may be essential to a healthy brain.

According to *Think Smart* author Richard Restak, obesity is more often associated with cognitive impairment than age, gender, education, or IQ.[5]

GLASBERGEN

Copyright 2008 by Randy Glasbergen.

CHIPS

"If the brain is mostly made of fat, then gaining weight in college helps you get smarter!"

A bigger waistline has also been associated with a smaller brain. A study at the University of Pittsburgh School of Medicine showed that the brain of an overweight person appeared 16 years older than the brain of a normal-weight person![6]

Results from a new imaging study reveal that, on average, obese subjects had 8% lower brain volume than normal-weight subjects, and overweight subjects had 4% lower brain volume.

A study at the Karolinska Institute in Stockholm found that participants who had been overweight in middle age had an 80% higher risk of being diagnosed with dementia in later life. Obese people, those having a body mass index (BMI) of 30 or above, had an almost four times higher risk of dementia.[7]

CHAPTER 5
Physical Movement – Activity is Activating

*"Those who think they have not time for bodily exercise
will sooner or later have to find time for illness."*

Edward Stanley

Good circulation is critical to get the power ingredients glucose and oxygen to the brain to fulfill our energy requirements. According to *Brain Rules* author John Medina, after about 10 minutes of sitting and listening to a presentation, our brain thinks it is vacation time.[1] Our cognitive performance drops down, our breath rate and circulation become impaired, and we sink into a relatively unhealthy and unproductive condition.

For instance, the longer people sit, the higher their risk of many health problems. A study published in the *American Journal of Epidemiology* showed that among 123,000 adults followed over 14 years, those who sat more than six hours a day were at least 18 percent more likely to die than those who sat less than three hours a day.[2]

There is no doubt that modern conveniences make life easier in many ways. In fact, at this point in history you can probably accomplish just about anything from the comfort of your couch: shopping, reading, watching movies, talking with friends, playing games, ordering food, doing research – even dating can now be done virtually, without having to move a muscle.

But, as human beings, we were built to be active. It is estimated that our Paleolithic ancestors had to walk 5–10 miles on an average day just to find food and shelter. Our bodies are genetically predisposed to frequent, consistent whole-body movement, but today we have reduced physical activity to seriously low levels. Why is regular movement so important as part of your daily strategy?

- Simple physical activity such as walking enhances breathing and increases heart rate, which enhances blood flow, energy production, and waste removal.

- Exercise stimulates the production of many different hormones necessary for cognitive functioning, in addition to changing the actual structure of the brain. For example, BDNF – our 'Miracle-Gro' for the brain – is boosted through aerobic exercise.

- Regular exercise also increases the amount and capacity of blood vessels in the brain. Unfortunately, despite all the people we think we see working hard in the gym, only about 5% of people even get the minimum amounts of exercise recommended for good health.

Our ancient survival instincts, so valuable thousands of years ago, continue to steer us to conserve energy – in other words, to eat more and move less. In order to make physical activity something we move toward instead of away from, we must consciously train our brain to consider movement as a daily benefit that's worth making the upfront energy investment.

To see a video of author Heidi Hanna talking about movement for brain health and performance, scan the QR code below

Exercise Strengthens the Brain

According to a large body of evidence, aerobic exercise increases and strengthens neuronal connections, increases the number of capillaries supplying glucose and oxygen to the brain, feeds the brain neurotrophins (chemical messengers) that enhance growth and connections, and promotes new cell growth, or neurogenesis.

Considering the fact that as adults we lose about 5-7% of brain volume each decade, the gains from exercise become critical just to maintain our current functioning. Fortunately, it doesn't take decades to see the benefit of exercise on the brain.

In 2007, German researchers found that people learned vocabulary words 20 percent faster following exercise than they did before exercise, and that the rate of learning correlated directly with levels of BDNF (Brain-derived Neurotrophic Factor, aka Miracle-Gro).[3] Also, cell growth can be seen after only six months of exercising just three times a week. In scans, the exercisers' brains looked as if they were two to three years younger than they actually were.[4]

Exercise improves learning by increasing alertness, attention, and motivation, and by enhancing the physical structure of the brain through the development of new cells and stronger connections between them.

Cognitive Fitness Benefits

Exercise has been shown to increase cognitive functions such as memory, learning, and overall quality of life. A study at the University of California, San Francisco showed that women who were more active had less cognitive decline than those who were sedentary.[5]

Not only did the group who walked about 17 miles a week (or about 45 minutes of walking, five days a week) maintain better cognitive functioning, researchers also found that every extra mile walked per week seemed to decrease the risk of cognitive decline by 13%, proving that every step counts.

A 2004 University of Illinois study found that people with high levels of aerobic fitness showed greater activation in key brain regions during performance of cognitive tasks compared with their less fit counterparts.[6]

According to Dr. Medina, a little bit of exercise goes a long way. Studies show that participating in some form of exercise just twice a week will give you benefits. "Bump it up to a 20-minute walk each day," he says, "and you will cut your risk of having a stroke – one of the leading causes of mental disability in the elderly – by 57%."[1]

Exercise is Medicine

Exercise also impacts the brain indirectly because it reduces the risk of other diseases. While it initially puts stress on the system, exercise ends up enhancing immune functioning because the small amount of stress stimulates the body to break down just a little bit, and then build back up stronger than before.

Numerous studies show that employees who exercise regularly take fewer sick days and spend less money on health claims. One company found that those who participated in their corporate exercise program took 80 percent fewer sick days. Another study showed that medical claims by employees who were members of a fitness center went down 27 percent, while nonmembers' claims rose by 17 percent.[7]

According to a report published in the late 1990s, health-care claims at a major beverage corporation averaged $500 less for employees per year who joined the company's fitness program compared with those who didn't.[8]

Heart disease is one of the largest killers in our world today. Exercise has been shown to increase healthy cholesterol in the blood stream, which helps to eliminate unhealthy cholesterol. Just 30 minutes three times a week has been shown to decrease blood pressure and increase the ability of the heart and lungs to optimize circulation. By utilizing sugar in the blood and increasing insulin sensitivity, exercise keeps triglycerides from clouding arteries and decreases the risk of developing diabetes.

Projections suggest that by the year 2020, 1 out of 2 people will have diabetes, which we know has a direct impact on brain health and functioning.

It is estimated that the risk of developing type 2 diabetes – the most common form of the disease, which results from a decrease in insulin efficiency – may be cut in half with just a 5–10% decrease in body fat.[9]

Specific Movement Recommendations

In order to have optimal circulation and energy throughout the day, here are some concrete movement suggestions to consider:

1. Aim to get up and move your body at least every 90 minutes. If you have meetings that last longer than 90 minutes, be sure to schedule stretch breaks. While you may have to sacrifice a few minutes of work, the return in energy will enable you to accomplish more in a shorter amount of time.

2. When it comes to regular exercise schedules, the American College of Sports Medicine recommends that individuals do moderate aerobic exercise for at least 30 minutes five days a week, or vigorous intensity exercise for at least 20 minutes three days a week.[10] Strength or resistance training should be performed at least two days a week. Stretching should be done everyday, if possible, ideally after exercise when the muscles are warm.

3. Make sure you do vigorous exercise, within your limits. Most people focus on the hours they spend at the gym or the number of reps or sets they do and wonder why they're not seeing results. When it comes to strategic exercise, intensity is key! A 2002 study

by the American Medical Association showed that a reduction in heart disease risk was linked to the intensity of exercise, not the amount of time spent working out.[11]

4. Consider playing a sport. One of the best ways to make exercise something you can stick with over time is to make it fun. In animal studies, forced exercise did not have the cognitive benefits of voluntary exercise. So pushing yourself to be miserable in the gym won't likely give you much of an advantage. (This may be due to the fact that the negative impact of stress hormones cancels out the benefits from exercise.)

5. Make regular physical activity a priority by putting it in a schedule, and keeping a firm appointment with yourself. The time of day that you exercise is not important; what is important is that you make time to exercise.

"The handle on your recliner does not count as an exercise machine."

CHAPTER 6
Stress Management –
Balancing Stress Balances Life

*"Our greatest weapon against stress
is our ability to choose one thought over another."*

William James

When we talk about stress management, many people assume that the goal should be to eliminate sources of stress. However, stress is not the enemy. In fact, life without stress would be a life without growth. Moderate periodic stress pushes us to do our best and be optimally fit.

It's often shocking to people to hear that one of the highest spikes in human mortality comes within about six months of retirement. Most people work hard their whole life, looking forward to the time when they can relax and enjoy the fruits of their labors. But our physical system is not designed to function in a state of all-or-nothing.

At its most basic, stress is anything that provokes change. A stressor can be internal (a challenging thought, for instance, or a recurrent memory) or external (a time deadline, a lecture to deliver, a date to go on). A stressor can be something negative, but it can also be something positive.

When it comes to your body and brain, negative stress can be thought of as anything that throws you out of balance. When you become out of sync, you will naturally do what you can to try to compensate in order to regain homeostasis. These internal efforts can be seen in the body chemistry as a shift in metabolic functioning in areas such as our immune system, glucose regulation, and hormone production, with some hormones getting turned on and others turned off.

Stress is all about initiating change, and change is a necessary part of life. Therefore your body and brain are well equipped to handle a significant amount of stress. The problem occurs when stress gets too great in volume, or too intense or long-term in nature, and your system becomes overwhelmed.

From a medical perspective, your brain is biologically able to deal effectively with stress that lasts about 30 seconds. Based on how your brain perceives stress, your body will produce different hormones designed to help stimulate your 'fight, flight, or freeze' response.

Stress that is immediate (or acute) only lasts for a short period of time, but chronic stress stimulates the prolonged secretion of hormones like cortisol that are not quickly flushed through your system, and can cause long-term damage.

Cortisol is so toxic to the brain that it can kill brain cells on contact.[1] According to stress researcher Robert Sapolsky, "For the vast majority of beasts on this planet, stress is about a short-term crisis, after which it's either over with or you're over with."[2] But for us humans, stress can last for days, months, or years at a time, giving cortisol hormones plenty of time to linger in our system, causing major damage.

When stress levels become too much for the brain to handle, deficits can be seen to virtually every kind of cognition: memory and executive function, motor skills, immune response, sleep, and mental/emotional health.

Researchers have studied elite performers in sports to determine how the brain works during times of peak performance. A recent article in *Golf Digest* discussed a study evaluating the brain activity of rookies vs. longtime pros. The more stressed amateur golfers showed higher activity levels in the areas of the brain that control our survival-based functioning (the limbic system), whereas the pros didn't have as much activity in that area. This highlights the difference between a 'clutch' brain and a stressed brain.[3]

I recently had an opportunity to speak with golf legend Sir Nick Faldo, and I asked him what he did to achieve peak performance when it mattered most. Nick told me that he used "verbal commands" to focus on what he wanted to do, and then on how he was going to do it. Rather than being distracted with negative thoughts, he stayed focused on the positive.

Nick also utilized visualization (which we will talk about more in the strength-training section) to 'see' himself hitting just the right shot.

"One of the problems with mental coaching is that many people think they have the one right solution for what everyone should do," he told me. "There is no right or wrong way; you just have to find what works for you, and that will be the correct way."

To see a video of author Heidi Hanna talking about
Biofeedback for stress management, scan the QR code below

Stress and Oxygen Deprivation

Prolonged stress, especially when combined with worry and anxiety, constricts the breathing muscles and reduces oxygen intake. Do you notice your short, shallow breathing when you are tense? And after a short period of time, being stuck in anxiety and stress can definitely make you feel dizzy due to a decrease in oxygen uptake.

When you find yourself habitually slipping into stressed breathing, the solution is not to push harder and do more. This will only continue to reduce your mental performance and clarity, not to mention your flexibility and creativity.

The recovery plan is to remember the *SHARP* Recharge Process and shift from tension mode to relaxation mode.

You must remember that even though short bouts of stress boost performance and memory, long-term stress is consistently dulling your mind. When you are under too much stress for too long, the wise recovery strategy is to remember to 'stop doing anything' for at least a short time, as we've been exploring in the first few exercises in this book.

One of the most challenging things for busy professionals to do is to add a recovery strategy to their routine. For some reason it's much easier for us to do something than not do anything. Blame it on the busyness of our world, constant access to technology, or the need to be connected 24/7 – resting is hard work!

For many people it's really uncomfortable to just be still. But like other healthy habits we want to form, relaxation is something that needs to be practiced in order to become more routine. Meditation, music, massage, hobbies, walking outside – the key is figuring out what works for you.

Just like anything that's not practiced regularly, relaxation can be quite challenging. We are so used to rushing around at a busy pace that many of us have developed 'stress addiction,' and experience major withdrawal when we try to slow down.

Studies on stress show that even negative situations can cause a rush of positive endorphins in the brain. Why? Endorphins are designed to help us cope with an emergency by stimulating some of the same areas involved with rewarding us for positive behavior. Lose this rush and you can find yourself feeling temporarily sluggish and unmotivated.

If you feel addicted to stress, you just might be!

This doesn't mean that you're doomed for gloom. It just means that relaxation and recovery are going to take even more effort and careful planning to incorporate into your routine. Practice recovery techniques regularly, use audio and video guides to support your relaxation practice, manage your energy expenditure more consistently throughout the day, and you'll find yourself less and less dependent on the stress rush to keep you going.

Self-Care Must Be Scheduled

In order to be helpful to those around us, we must first take care of ourselves. People pour their blood, sweat, and tears into a career that often uses up all of their energy, and say that they "do it all for their family." But almost always, what their family wants most from them is not more *from* them, but more *of* them!

To pour everything you have into providing for others, but not be fully present when you're with them, can leave people feeling neglected, despite all of your efforts.

What people want most from you is your energy and engagement, both of which require you to replenish your energy regularly. Scheduling time to take care of yourself isn't something that can get pushed aside if you want to be your best self for the people and things that matter most to you.

Stress Strategy: Summary

Life is full of stress for most of us – and in itself, stress is not bad. Two people can be in the same stressful situation and yet can react in entirely different ways.

You are constantly deciding how to respond to the challenges in your life. Learning how to keep your cool, and how to regain inner equilibrium when you lose your cool, is one of the most important cognitive abilities you can develop.

We have seen that prolonged stress grabs at your breathing, reduces the oxygen flow to your brain, and burns up your vital brain chemicals too quickly, leaving you to crash afterwards. The good news is that you have the ability to train yourself so that your response to external stressors is healthy.

You can also learn to more effectively quiet your self-generated internal stressors (all those worried thoughts and anxious imaginings inside your own mind) that hold you in stress mode all day.

Throughout this book we'll be returning to this important theme of regularly taking a Recharge Break to recover, rebalance, and rejuvenate your energy and engagement.

Copyright 2006 by Randy Glasbergen, www.glasbergen.com

"I'm finally learning how to relax.
Unfortunately, relaxation makes me tense."

CHAPTER 7
Sleep – Resting is Working

"Sleep is not a vast wasteland of inactivity.
The sleeping brain is highly active at various times during the night,
performing numerous physiological, neurological,
and biochemical housekeeping tasks."

Dr James B. Maas

According to the National Sleep Foundation, approximately 70 million Americans are affected by chronic sleep loss or sleep disorders. The annual costs associated with chronic sleep loss are estimated at $16 billion in health care expenses and $150 billion in lost productivity.[1]

Sleep deprivation and sleepiness have obvious and subtle adverse effects on performance, response times, accuracy, attention, and concentration.

Lack of quality sleep has been associated with a wide range of quality-of-life measures, such as social functioning, mental and physical health, and even early death.[2]

In one of my workshops I spoke with a physician who was struggling with sleep deprivation. He told me that he had recently been pulled over by the police twice in one evening on suspicion of driving under the influence, when in fact he was driving under the influence of too little sleep.

Considering the fact that people who are suffering from lack of sleep perform just as poorly as people who are drunk in driving simulation tests, maybe we should start penalizing those who are sleepy at the wheel.

The area of the brain that may be most affected by sleep, or the lack of it, is the prefrontal cortex. This area is responsible for your 'executive functioning' processes such as learning, judgment, reasoning, memory consolidation, and understanding.

In his book *Sleep for Success*, Dr. James Maas states that someone who is sleep-deprived is operating with about 50% less memory ability.[3] Maas says that the final two hours of sleep are crucial for memories to become fixed in the brain. It is during this time that most of us experience REM sleep, when the events of the day are replayed over and over again to become stored in our mental filing cabinet.

Studies with animals and humans suggest that brain activity occurring during the day is reactivated during sleep as your brain is consolidating memory. Just like the muscles in your body, the connections in your brain require rest to do the work of forming stronger pathways, repairing, and rebuilding.

A friend of mine, Admiral Ray Smith, served as a Navy Seal for 31 years and commander of the Seals for four years. We spoke recently about lessons he learned from his time in the Navy and throughout his decades of athletic competition. One of the primary life changes he made as he gained experience was to his sleep routine.

"I remember when I was young, I'd focus on maximizing the amount of time I spent working, training, or competing," he said. "As I have gotten older, I notice more and more the impact of sleep on my cognitive functioning, and I will not compromise sleep."

Sleepy Body, Sleepy Brain

Numerous studies show the impact of sleep deprivation on performance and health. For instance, according to the National Institutes of Health, sleeping less than 6 hours can have a serious effect on your ability to think and act properly the following day, even if you feel subjectively as though you are continuing to function at normal levels.[4]

In a study at the University of Pennsylvania, researchers found that subjects who slept 4-6 hours a night for 14 consecutive nights showed deficits in cognitive performance equivalent to how they would perform after going without sleep for up to three days in a row.[5]

Lack of sleep has also been correlated with obesity, increases in smoking and alcohol use, chronic inactivity, heart disease, blood-sugar imbalances, and increases in stress hormones such as adrenaline and cortisol.[6]

Sleep is the body's natural recovery phase. If you eliminate the necessary balancing process achieved when you sleep well, your entire system becomes out of balance at core levels, and you will experience adverse symptoms in a variety of physical, emotional, and mental ways.

How Much is Enough?

The amount of sleep that is optimal for brain health and performance is unique to each individual. To determine how much sleep you need, find out how much time it takes for you to wake up feeling refreshed, without needing an alarm clock. Studies show that most humans need 7-9 hours of sleep each night, which is why you've most likely heard the recommendation for an average of 8 hours each night.

However, some people can function well with 6 or 7 hours of sleep while other people need 9 to 10. According to recent research, dipping below the 6-hour mark impairs cognitive functioning for just about everyone, so it is recommended that you always get at least 6 hours of quality sleep each night.

Signs That You're Not Getting Enough Sleep

1. You're dependent on an alarm clock. If you're getting enough sleep, you should usually be able to wake up on time without a morning alarm.

2. You're drowsy while driving. Feeling drowsy at the wheel is a sure sign that you're too tired – and it's also very dangerous.

3. You're attached to the coffee pot. A cup of coffee to start your day is fine, but you shouldn't have to rely on coffee, or other energy drinks, to stay alert.

4. You're making mistakes. It's harder to focus and concentrate when you are tired. You're more easily distracted and less likely to catch and fix errors.

5. You're forgetful. Sleep loss may explain why you have a hard time remembering things. Sleep deprivation hinders short-term memory.

6. You're snippy and irritable. Being tired can have a negative effect on your moods. It makes you more likely to feel depressed, anxious, and frustrated.

7. You're frequently sick. Without sleep your immune system is not at full strength, and it's harder for your body to fight illness.

To Sleep Well at Night, Take Breaks During the Day

As we discussed in the section on stress management, oscillating between action and relaxation is important. Instead of seeing our day as one long full-steam-ahead marathon, breaking it up into smaller chunks allows you not only to stay more focused, but also to get strategic recovery breaks that will improve your ability to recharge effectively and efficiently.

By incorporating relaxation strategies throughout the day, as you're learning in this book, you keep stress levels down so that at the end of the day you aren't trying to fall asleep with an overdose of adrenaline and other stimulating hormones in your system.

You can't go at light speed all day long and expect your system to come to a screeching halt once you crawl into bed. Even if you utilize healthy sleep rituals, limit caffeine, and turn off distractions at night, your brain can't immediately turn off just because you tell it to after going at a hectic pace all day.

The Importance of Sleep Rituals

Have you ever tried to read a book before bed? If you're like most people, you only made it through a few pages and probably read the same section over and over again. There are several reasons why reading helps to induce sleep. It shifts your attention away from stressful thoughts of the day, and it may provide relaxation through entertainment.

But the driving force behind this phenomenon is the natural brain training that occurs as a result of repeatedly connecting a place (bed), an activity (reading), and a desired outcome (falling asleep).

You can derive similar results with other strategies that utilize the same principles. For example, you can regularly take a bath or shower before bed, listen to relaxing music, do some quiet yoga, go for a short walk, or make a cup of herbal tea – and you will soon associate the ritual with getting sleepy. Any mind-calming, body-relaxing activity you begin to do at bedtime will enhance your ability to fall into deep sleep.

More Sleep Strategies

Some activities are important to avoid before bedtime. Others can assist you in falling asleep and staying asleep long enough to feel rested. Here are a few tips for sleeping well:

- *Go to bed early.* Studies suggest that early to bed and early to rise is more suited for our natural rhythms.

- *Don't watch drama or the news.* Any stimulation of emotional tension or excitement will fill your system with anti-sleep hormones.

106

- *Learn to let go of upsetting thoughts and emotions.* Practice meditation or another technique for calming and quieting your thinking mind so that you are feeling content and in harmony at bedtime.

- *Focus on the present moment, not the past or the future.* Sleep comes to you when you're fully relaxed in your body in the present moment. Use meditation as we're learning in this book to bring your attention fully and enjoyably into the moment.

- *Get out of bed.* Rather than tossing and turning in bed, if you're having trouble falling asleep, get out of bed and do something relaxing until you feel sleepy.

- *Limit naps.* If you take a nap during the day, keep it brief. Nap for less than an hour and before 3 p.m.

- *Wake up early on the weekend.* It is best to go to bed and wake up at the same times on the weekend as you do during the workweek. This enables you to build a steady pattern around your sleep schedule.

- *Avoid late-day caffeine.* Avoid caffeine in the afternoon and at night. It stays in your system for hours and can make it hard for you to fall asleep.

- *Adjust the lights.* Dim the lights in the evening so your body knows it will soon be time to sleep. Let in the sunlight in the morning to boost your alertness.

- *Wind down.* Take some time to wind down before going to bed. Get away from the computer, turn off the TV and your cell phone, and relax quietly for 15–30 minutes. Parents should keep TVs and computers out of their children's bedrooms.

- *Eat a little.* Never eat a large meal right before bedtime. While a big meal may cause you to feel drowsy, your body will have to work hard to process all of that food, which can actually be stimulating to your system. Enjoy a healthy snack or light dessert so you don't go to bed hungry.

- *Avoid alcohol.* A drink or two may help you fall asleep, but it may also keep you from getting the quality of sleep you need. Alcohol is quickly metabolized by the body and has a stimulating effect on the brain, disrupting sleep even when you don't notice yourself waking up.

To access a pre-sleep guided meditation track,
scan the QR code below

"I toss and turn all night and you won't count
that as an eight-hour aerobic workout?!"

CHAPTER 8
Connection – Social Support is Life Support

"If you want to go fast, go alone.
If you want to go far, go together."

African proverb

Finally, we come to what might be the most critical indicator of long-term health and fulfillment; your inner sense of adequate emotional and social connection. With all the technological advances we have to keep us connected across the globe, one might assume that we are more social than ever. However, this constant preoccupation with staying connected has in certain ways actually torn apart the concept of relationship as we once knew it.

Keep in mind that social connection is based on how you feel, not necessarily on the number of friends you have or whether you're married or single. It's the strength of your relationships - the depth of the emotional bonds - that's most important.

A recent study examined data from more than 309,000 people and found that a lack of strong relationships increased the risk of premature death from all causes by 50% – an effect comparable to smoking up to 15 cigarettes a day, and greater than obesity and physical inactivity.[1]

George Vaillant, director for 40 years of the Harvard project "The Study of Adult Development," states there are "70 years of evidence that our relationships with other people matter, and matter more than anything else in the world."[2]

Loneliness Is Bad for Your Health

When it comes to our survival instincts, being part of a supportive group may be one of the most important strategies to keeping us alive and fulfilled. Researchers can trigger the physiological stress response in animals simply by removing them from their social structure; isolation activates stress hormones. And the same is true in humans – loneliness is a threat to survival.

In their book *Loneliness: Human Nature and the Need for Social Connection,* John Cacioppo and William Patrick argue that loneliness, like hunger, is an alarm signal that evolved hundreds of thousands of years ago when group cohesion was essential to fight off attacks.[3]

In a study with children, students were divided into small groups and asked to enjoy some bite-sized cookies. Before tasting the cookies, some groups were told that no one wanted to work with their group, while other groups were told that everyone wanted to work with them. Each student was then handed a plate of cookies. In the groups that were told everyone wanted to work with them, students ate an average of 4.5 cookies, but in the 'rejected' groups they ate 9 apiece.

The authors of the study asked, "Is it any wonder we turn to ice-cream when we're sitting at home feeling all alone in the world?"[3]

As research continues to look at the relevance of social connections, a new field of social science has emerged. Social neuroscience looks at the associations between social and neural connections, and determines the impact of our relationships on health and well-being.

Dr. Cacioppo and Dr. Gary Berntson have been credited with founding the social neuroscience movement. By evaluating brain scans and monitoring physiological responses, Cacioppo and Berntson found that there was a dramatic influence of social context, or a sense of connection, on the brain and the body. In fact, the impact was so intense that they were able to see changes to the genetic expression in white blood cells. Their research demonstrated that loneliness can cause increases in blood pressure, stress, depression, anxiety, and cortisol production.

Loneliness affects immune functioning negatively, impairs quality sleep, and has been correlated to the risk of developing Alzheimer's disease. And loneliness can be a vicious cycle, in that it can trigger a sense of sadness that causes more isolation and an even greater sense of loneliness.

Feeling lonely changes behavior as well. Studies have connected loneliness with a decrease in exercise frequency, an increase in caloric consumption (specifically comfort foods high in processed carbohydrates), and an increase in alcohol and drug consumption (both prescription and illegal).[3]

Of course, most of us have wonderful and deeply-meaningful experiences during solitary times as well, and there are people who enjoy being alone most of the time and don't need a social group in order to feel happy and fulfilled. But for most people, experts agree that relationships may be the most important contributor to overall life satisfaction and emotional well-being among people of all ages and cultures.[4] As it turns out, it seems most good times in life happen not in isolation, but with companions.

Connection Boosts the Mind and Body

Recent research has shown something quite interesting related to mental performance and social connectedness. In 2008, Ybarra and colleagues evaluated the social engagement of 3,600 people aged 24 to 96 and found that the more connected people felt, the better they performed on a mental exam.[5]

Why? One explanation is because when you experience a positive social connection, your brain releases a feel-good chemical called oxytocin, a hormone that almost instantly reduces anxiety and improves focus and concentration.[6]

Research by Dr. Larry Dossey and others have shown that people who receive emotional support during a healing process demonstrate statistically improved chances of recovery.

Heart attack survivors are three times more likely to survive when they receive support[7], and women participating in a breast-cancer support group doubled life expectancy post-surgery[8].

At-work studies have shown another positive benefit of feeling connected. In a Gallup well-being study, it was found that employees who had a 'best friend' at work were seven times more likely to feel engaged with their job than those without this connection. Furthermore, the connected employees also exhibited higher sales and profitability, engaged customers better, produced higher quality work, had greater commitment to the firm's mission, had better safety records, were happier at work, and had a higher chance of sticking with a firm. Of the workers who didn't have a best friend at work, only 8% were engaged in their job.[9] These are quite remarkable statistics showing the positive power of feeling connected at work!

Quantity vs. Quality

Many people these days have tens or even hundreds of 'friends' on Facebook and other social media groups. The problem with being overly connected, as you may have realized if you're an avid social networker, is that it's impossible to maintain a true depth of connection with so many people. Social-networking websites and tools are great for expanding your quantity of connections, but you will quickly see that it's impossible to keep up with what every single friend is doing.

What really matters is the quality of our relationships. In fact, many people have only a few friends but feel fully engaged socially. While marriage was once thought to help people feel connected, it turns out that it's the quality of the relationship (no surprise here), not marital status, which determines the potential benefit.

To see a video of author Heidi Hanna talking about the importance of social connections, scan the QR code below

Building Better Relationships

One of the best ways to strengthen existing relationships is to dedicate focused time to people you care about. My clients often complain about not having enough time to spend with the people they love. I like to remind them that it's not necessarily about the time we are able to share, but the quality of the energy we bring to the time we have.

We often forget that it's our full attention that people want most. We've all experienced times when we've been physically present and completely absent mentally or emotionally. We've also all had occasions when we didn't have much time available but managed to have an extraordinary experience because we were fully focused in the moment.

To increase your sense of connection, you might want to take a look at your current schedule and identify times when you could reach out to someone for a conversation, or ask them to join you on a task or activity. This is a great opportunity for mental 'cross training'

Grab a friend or colleague to go for a walk so you can exercise while you connect. Or ask a family member to join you for a movie so you can improve your connection with them while getting some relaxation (if you chose the right movie, and the right family member, of course).

Take seriously the fact that when it comes to your relationships, there is nothing that people want more from you than your full loving attention – right here, right now.

Being Alone But Not Feeling Lonely

Although relationships are incredibly enriching, being alone doesn't have to be lonely – which is a good thing, considering how many of us are in fact alone. The latest Census figures indicate there are some 31 million Americans living alone, which accounts for more than a quarter of all US households. The issue isn't whether you're living alone, but whether you're feeling lonely or satisfied with your solitary situation.

There are certainly many benefits to being on your own:

1. Quality time in solitude can help you to unwind and recharge so that you have more energy to give to the people around you.

2. Studies highlight the benefit of isolation for certain cognitive functions such as memory (we can concentrate more when we think we're alone), empathy (taking time to think through how others may feel), focus (decreasing multitasking), and judgment (not being influenced by other's perspectives).

3. Insights and important realizations, even the feeling of connectedness with a higher power or sense of purpose, come to us most readily when we're alone rather than caught up in socializing.

According to sociological estimations, we are much more extroverted now than ever before. In traditional times, when most people lived pastoral lives, human beings spent much more time alone than in our modern times. But just being surrounded by people doesn't guarantee a sense of connection or belonging.

It is our personal perspective that carries the most weight when it comes to how our relationships influence our brain.

While staying socially active is definitely an important part of brain health, working on your inner perception of your sense of connectedness with others can also decrease feelings of loneliness, especially at times when you may not be as connected as you would like.

"If a tree falls in the forest, but you don't hear about it on Facebook, MySpace, YouTube or Twitter, did it really happen?"

Training Exercise #4: Feeling Connected

You can actively nurture your sense of connectedness, with yourself, with your deeper spiritual source of energy, and with others you care about, by focusing your attention in these directions and using the basic tools of meditation to wake up the power of mutual love and interconnectedness. If this possibility appeals to you, here's a short meditation aiming in this direction:

As we did before, begin by gently turning your mind's focus of attention, even while reading these words, to the sensations of the air flowing in and out of your nose. Tune into the movements in your chest and belly as you breathe without any effort at all. Just set your breathing free, and expand your awareness to include your whole body, here in this present moment.

Now, see what feeling and experience comes to you when you say this focus statement to yourself:

"I feel deep love for myself, just as I am."

For a few breaths, open up to feel your inner sense of loving yourself, without any negative thoughts or judgments.

And now let this feeling of love and oneness expand within you, as you open your heart to experience your connection with God (Higher Power, Universe) by saying:

"I feel one in my heart with God."

And with that wonderful sense of connection vibrant within you, bring to mind someone you know and care for – see their face in your mind's eye – and see what feeling and experience comes to you when you say this third focus statement to this person, as if they are here with you right now:

"I feel warm love and connectedness with you right now."

PART THREE

Real-World Brain Training

TRAINING YOUR BRAIN

Training your brain is similar in many ways, as we've seen, to training your physical body. However, as you've also been discovering in this book, training your brain is a unique challenge because it can at times seem so simple and subtle, which can lead us to assume it's not that important.

Your brain is where you actually experience yourself as alive and present and full of feelings, thoughts, memories, imaginations, and all the rest.

In this section, we're going to bring together everything we've talked about thus far, and see how you can approach training your brain in the real world.

A key element of cognitive fitness is the ability of your brain to focus mental energy and attention on the things that matter most to you, in order to maximize your health, happiness, and performance. And as we've seen, just like in physical fitness, mental fitness requires several complementary elements of training in order to optimize:

- **Strength**

- **Flexibility**

- **Endurance**

In the chapters that follow, we'll discuss these dimensions of fitness in more detail, including why each is important and how specifically you can train to make improvements. Each section will have suggestions and exercises with real-world applications, including:

- 'top techniques' for each training target

- 'sprint workout' options that only require 30 seconds to 2 minutes of training time

- the 'training takeaway' that highlights the key points of that section

CHAPTER 9
Strength Training – Building Mental Muscle

A strong brain will allow you to focus your mental energy where you want it, when you want it, with maximum clarity and precision. Focus is at the core of mental performance, so developing your ability to invest attention exactly where you need it most will be key to consistent mental strength.

Multitasking is the enemy of peak performance because it takes your mental energy and spreads it out in several directions at once, thus reducing your focus on any one target.

Unfortunately, for most people the natural tendency to multitask, trained by years of operating this way, often overrides the need to focus on one thing at a time. A strong brain is able to fully engage and aim the power of your attention, rather than getting distracted by everything else that's going on around you.

To see a video of author Heidi Hanna talking about 'distraction resistance' for mental strength, scan the QR code below

Strength Training

Building mental muscle in this regard requires regularly doing basic resistance training with your mind by choosing a particular target, holding that focus for a period of time, and resisting the distractions around you. This is similar to how you might train a muscle by doing resistance training, pushing or pulling a weight against the force of gravity.

You can choose to focus on anything. The key is to discipline yourself to hold that resistance posture for a certain amount of time without your attention drifting elsewhere.

One of the most effective focusing exercises, as we've seen, is to spend just a few minutes directing your attention to your breath experience, without drifting into thought.

For thousands of years, the ancient Yogic tradition has taught practitioners this core mental exercise because it accomplishes so much in just one process:

- you strengthen your ability to focus

- you turn inward and regain your senses in the present moment

- you let go of thoughts that generate stress and fatigue

You can also pause and focus on anything else you want to for resistance training. For instance, you can focus on counting from 1 to 24, with one count for each breath, or from 1 to 12 and then back to 1 again.

The challenge is to keep your mind focused on the present moment, rather than drifting off into past or future thoughts, or being distracted by your environment.

You can also focus on a single visual object for a certain period of time, or for a certain number of counts. Or just look out the window at a particular unmoving object, and hold your focus there. Holding focus is the key. You will strengthen your ability to focus in general, so that no matter what you're doing you will be able to bring your best mental energy to what matters most to you in that moment.

Beyond Information Overload

With so many electronic ways to stay connected to the outside world these days, it's easy to find yourself feeling overloaded with information. Studies show that the younger you are, the less likely you even realize that you are constantly being bombarded with information and mental stimuli. It's become the universal norm to be overwhelmed by data of all kinds and levels of quality.

And this is a fairly recent phenomenon. Back in my day (never thought I'd hear myself say that), we had to get up and change the channel on the TV every time we wanted to watch a different show; the only people with cell phones or pagers were doctors and (so I heard) drug dealers; and if you wanted to read a book or use a computer, you went to the library.

Nowadays of course we have a 24/7 connection to almost anything we want via a multitude of networks on our smartphones, iPads, and laptop computers – even while flying in the friendly skies. It's not uncommon to see elementary kids carrying around their own digital devices. My 6-year-old nephew and 4-year-old niece both seem to intuitively know how to use the same iPad that I still have yet to figure out after a couple of years.

But while all this technology makes life easier, it also creates a big problem. We have quickly become addicted to the constant electronic 'noise' and too often hardly pay any attention to what's happening right around us or within our own body.

I recently had an opportunity to go to a remote spa retreat with a good friend, and it was the first time in years that I was truly not able to stay connected. Cell phone reception was impossible, and the wireless internet connection they promised was erratic at best. On the third and final day my friend said, "Hey, I think you just got here." We both laughed, knowing how difficult it is to slow down when you're used to running at such a crazy, chaotic pace.

Consider this: How long does it take you to feel like you're on vacation when you've taken some time off? Two, three days? All week? Too often when we finally tune out the worry of what we might be missing, we immediately start worrying about all the work we'll be coming back to when we return. Or we convince ourselves that staying plugged in is better than having to try to catch up after the fact, so we never truly shut down at all.

When I returned to the real world I was shocked at how loud everything seemed. I could barely stand to have the TV on, and almost everything I saw on it made me feel depressed or anxious. Sitting in a restaurant trying to write, I could barely hear myself think over the loud music blaring over the speakers. And then ... I adjusted. Don't we all? Unless we've taken time to be quiet for a while, when we're in the middle of the noise, we usually don't even notice.

Why is this topic important to our cognitive fitness? Because although we may not realize it, constant environmental stimuli have been show to have a negative impact on our mental energy and functioning.

In a recent article on information overload, Derek Dean and Caroline Webb of McKinsey & Company compared too much mental stimulation to eating too much food.[1] Many people eat more than they need as a way to distract themselves from their problems, or from tasks they react to or just don't feel like dealing with. An overabundance of information can provide the same task distraction, which keeps people from paying attention to more important issues.

The authors suggest that this happens by flooding us "with a variety of questions and topics that frequently could be addressed by others," which can distract us from the unpleasant issues we most need to deal with.

The pull to be constantly on and constantly connected is a serious problem in the business world, as it quickly begins to wear away at the priceless human capital of clear, focused attention.

We all know that we need to protect and strategically manage our most valuable resources such as time and money, but we often burn through our mental capital like it's nothing, assuming it will always be there. In my workshops, this issue is a frequent topic of discussion, and oftentimes debate.

Employees complain that they have no choice but to stay attached to their technological leashes (cell phones, text messages, e-mails, instant messenger, etc). But is this really true? Are we being paid to focus on a job and get it done efficiently, correctly, and creatively, or to fixate on three things at once and not do anything really well?

The key issue here is the story or excuse that we tell ourselves that keeps us feeling so attached to all of these external inputs. Most people have convinced themselves that they must respond ASAP or something horrible is going to happen, but play that tape out all the way to see how the story ends. What will happen if we don't respond immediately? Other than a few of my clients who are physicians, life and work will go on for the majority of us, and meanwhile we'll be able to focus where we really do need all of our attention – here and now.

According to Dean and Webb, if we don't do something to change our current constantly distracted working norms, we are "...at risk of moving toward an ever less thoughtful and creative professional reality."[1]

My challenge to you, and the other the busy professionals I work with, is to determine who sets those instant reply expectations in the first place, and to change them if they're interfering with mental clarity and performance.

Consider this: If you respond within 2-3 minutes to every single e-mail, people will expect you to keep it up. But if you have an established pattern, or norm, that tells people they will hear back from you within 24 or even 48 hours, you might be surprised to find out that for the majority of e-mails this time frame is more than sufficient.

So – what can you do?

1. First of all, watch yourself for a while and see just how often you let yourself be distracted from your primary work. Be honest. Identify your existing habits, and the stories and excuses you hold in your mind telling you that it's important to let yourself be distracted.

2. Then start establishing discipline in your electronic life by turning off everything you can for a certain period of time, and only occasionally checking to see who's contacted you.

3. Also, consider talking with your supervisor about this issue and find out what the expectations truly are. Get permission to unplug from time to time. And if you work for yourself or are the boss, look at your own habits and story, and establish new rules and disciplines that will override distraction patterns that don't serve you.

4. Just say so to attention grabbers. Everybody wants your attention because it is your most valuable commodity. Where you spend this resource determines what you buy. So begin to JUST SAY NO to attention grabbers. Take charge of your own mind!

Resistance training for the brain is all about actively resisting the temptation to be distracted. Otherwise you don't have a chance, because all the new media gadgets are specifically designed to grab and temporarily possess your attention.

Multitasking and Your Monkey Brain

With so many demands on your mental attention and energy, it's easy to find yourself pulled in multiple directions. Jumping from one project to another may seem like the only option for getting things done; however, the negative impact on attention and focus is significant.

Although being good at multitasking is often part of a job description, you may want to change the way you look at multiple priorities, so that your mental energy can remain tightly focused on those things that really require your attention each moment.

Even though a single-focus approach may appear to take more time, the fact is that you are actually getting more quality work done in the time you have allotted, so you end up saving precious time in the long run, while also increasing your productivity and performance.

Perceptually, multitasking is a bit of a misnomer, because your brain is wired in a way that only allows it to focus on one thing at a time. As with juggling, it may appear that you're doing several tasks at once, but you can only focus on one ball at a time – the rest are just floating in the air without your attention at that moment.

Multitasking is actually switching focus here and there and back again very fast. And the time it takes to switch your attention back and forth causes you to lose time, make mistakes, and be much less efficient. Why? Because when we switch tasks, we have to turn our attention away from one task and then determine or recall the rules for completing the next task.

In a recent study, participants who completed two simultaneous tasks took up to 30 percent longer and made twice as many errors as those who completed the same tasks in sequence.[2]

Time-management experts report that in many business situations, it can take 10 to 20 minutes to fully recover from shifting attention, with the time increasing for more complex tasks.

Another problem with multitasking is that it forces you to respond quickly, without time to assess a situation, consider multiple options, and then mindfully make a decision. As mentioned earlier, this situation forces you to depend on your habit drive 'monkey brain' that's grounded in past experience and emotional reactions, rather than rational decision making. The result is more errors, faulty judgment, and a lack of present moment responsiveness.

Researchers at Reuters found that two-thirds of respondents felt that chronic 'information overload' had decreased job satisfaction and damaged their personal relationships. One-third believed it had damaged their health.[3]

The added stress of multitasking results in an increase in stress hormones, which can damage brain cells over time. People who are multitasking too much often experience various warning signs such as difficulty with short-term memory, inability to focus, or gaps in attentiveness.

Staying focused on one task at a time will also benefit your personal relationships because you will be more able to pay full attention to the people you are with. Friendships and other meaningful relationships are based on your ability to give someone you care about your full attention.

Multitasking every now and then is okay, especially when tasks aren't important. "You can do several things at the same time," says Dr. Marcel Just, co-director of Carnegie Mellon University's Center for Cognitive Brain Imaging. "But you're kidding yourself if you think you can do so without cost."[4]

Just remember to spend time regularly toning your distraction resistance muscles through focus practice, stress management, and a good self-care regimen that provides you with proper nutrition, physical activity, and adequate sleep.

Building Focus and Concentration

"The difference between passing time and spending time wisely depends on making smart choices about what to pay attention to."

Dan Siegel in Mindsight

Although many of us have trained ourselves to be decent multitaskers and often fall into this pattern due to automatic-pilot habits, we can create a new way of doing things by utilizing the training strategies of cognitive fitness. This doesn't necessarily require more effort, but a smarter strategy. In her book *Rapt*, Winifred Gallagher reminds us, "Most failures occur despite effort, not due to a lack of it."[5]

It's not about working longer hours or trying harder; it's about bringing the best energy that we have to the time we have. Mental focus and attention are crucial to making sure that happens.

An important consideration when it comes to our mental energy is the impact of constant stimuli on the brain. Because there are so many things competing for our attention at any particular time, it is the brain's job to determine what is important and what can be ignored. And this requires energy.

It turns out that focusing attention, especially when trying to demonstrate restraint or willpower, is a very energy-demanding activity. Recent studies by Baumeister and colleagues demonstrated that like a muscle, our ability to elicit self-control decreases in strength as it is used.[6]

The experiments consistently demonstrated two lessons:

1. **You have a finite amount of willpower that becomes depleted as you use it.**

2. **You use the same stock of willpower for all manner of tasks.**

A willpower shortage impacts not only your ability to focus attention on the people and things that matter to you, but it also wreaks havoc on your physical body. When people in laboratory experiments exercise mental self-control, their pulse becomes more erratic. Some experiments have shown that chronic physical pain leaves people with a perpetual shortage of willpower because their minds are so depleted by the struggle to ignore the pain.[6]

Imagine if you were paying attention to everything happening around you – you'd quickly develop an attention deficit. Your ability to automatically tune out the unnecessary is critical for your brain to maintain optimal functioning.

Right now you're focused consciously on the words you're reading. You're probably not aware of your heartbeat, most of the background sounds around you, the memory of what you did two weeks ago, or the imagination of what you're going to do tomorrow – and that's your brain working nonstop to help you keep focused on what's most important.

To be easily distracted is often a lack of intent and discipline, and you can train your brain to focus more diligently on what you're doing by practicing distraction resistance exercises, and literally building a stronger willpower muscle.

Distraction Resistance

What you do not pay attention to is probably more important than what you do pay attention to. Potential distractions are all around you, and your brain is hardwired to keep alert, just below the level of conscious awareness, to detect sounds and movements that might indicate danger of some sort in order to protect you from threats in your environment.

So it's wise to minimize extraneous sounds and visual distractions when you're working. Even little things in your environment can cause your brain to brain to jump from one thing to another to determine if the sound or movement is a sign of danger. And each slight interruption of your focus of attention will then cost you moments or even minutes to return your focus fully to your work.

According to a study by Gloria Mark at the University of California, Irvine, the average person working in an office spent only about three minutes on a task before being interrupted or purposefully shifting focus of attention to another task.[7]

And while it may feel like you are constantly being bombarded by distractions from other people, nearly half the time it was the person being studied who independently chose to focus his or her attention on something new.[8]

Most jobs require shifting periodically to a number of different types of work. Life would be a bit boring if we had to do just one task all the time. It can be quite difficult to manage multiple priorities throughout the day, so coming up with a solid task-management process is critical. (A popular resource for many of my clients has been David Allen's method, described in his book *Getting Things Done.*[9])

What To Do: When it comes to training your brain to focus on the task at hand, I recommend using a 'turn off and tune out' philosophy.

A: Turn it off: Purposefully go around and eliminate any unnecessary noise that might be fighting for your brain's attention. This could be actual noise, such as a TV or radio running in the background, or conversations going on around you. I'm not suggesting you tell everyone around you to shut up, (it doesn't work well, I've tried), but you can often 'turn it off' by closing a door, or finding a quieter environment. Also turn off your e-mail, cell phone and other such attention grabbers for the duration of your work, or at least for a set timeframe. Keep in mind, putting your cell phone on vibrate still causes a distraction, so whenever you truly need to focus attention, try turning it off (if you can find the switch).

B: Tune it out: If you must stay put, that's when your focus training will prove beneficial because you will have practiced the ability to center your attention on what's important and ignore what isn't.

In his book *The Effective Executive*, Peter Drucker adds one more step to this turn it off and tune it out approach – take time out.[10] He emphasizes the need for us to give our brain time to shut down for a while, and reminds us that we do some of our best work when we're not trying to.

This became obvious to me early on in my career when I found myself having my best ideas while getting a massage. There was something about being able to totally disengage and actively work on shutting down my mind that allowed my creativity to soar. I actually started taking a notepad with me for those creative moments so I didn't have to worry about trying to remember everything, which had been causing my stress levels to rise up once again, defeating the purpose of the massage.

Use a 'Focus Phrase'

Similar to mantras, which help us focus our mind on the positive, a 'focus phrase' is a word or series of words that you can use to center your mind on what's most important to you in the moment. One of my favorite examples: In the movie *For the Love of the Game*, Kevin Costner's character was pitching in a big game and being heckled quite obnoxiously. With the world around him in chaos, Costner said to himself, "Clear the mechanism." At that point the bothersome sounds go away, and Costner is left with the quiet hush of his own mind, which he had trained to stay focused on only what was important in that moment – just him and the glove.

I no doubt identify with this film because of my experience as a softball pitcher for so many years. I remember what it was like to feel the rush of going into the game with two outs and the bases loaded while the other team cheered annoyingly. My catcher and I came up with some pretty funny sayings to help me focus on just her and the glove (I will keep those to myself to protect the innocent and the guilty.)

The brain has often been compared to a computer. What happens when you have too many programs operating at one time? The computer slows down, may freeze up, and could potentially crash. What happens when there is too much on our mind at one time? Similar results. From time to time we have to turn off our brain, reboot, and come back in order to be focused and energized.

Nowadays I use a different kind of focus phrase to help me concentrate on the present moment - whether I'm with a client, a friend, or a family member. I often tell myself, "Be here, now." I recently had a client tell me about another great one, "Clear and present." This individual, and his team at work, use the phrase to help them prepare before meetings. They have a quick discussion about anything that might be distracting one of the team members so that everyone has a clear mind and is able to be fully present in the meeting.

Associating particular words or phrases with specific situations is a good way to do mental strength training. Each time you connect two things in the brain, you release a chemical signal that makes that connection stronger. If you practice deep breathing, which triggers the relaxation response in the body, while at the same time repeating a phrase such as "relax and refocus," you associate that phrase with the response that's occurring as a result of the breathing.

The more you practice, the stronger that association becomes, and the quicker you're able to induce a positive state of mind with just a simple phrase.

As you repeat correlations over and over, you create a new automatic pilot. And by combining them with a desired response, you can begin to see a synergistic effect.

Repeating the phrase "Just have fun" before I do a presentation is one way I remind myself that when I have fun, I do a much better job. A couple of years ago I decided to add a visual symbol during my presentations, setting a small monkey (which represents fun to me) next to my time clock on the podium. If I became overly wrapped-up in the session, I would have an external cue to stay focused on what was most important to me in the moment – in this case, having fun – so that I would enjoy the process and not allow the stress of the situation to become overwhelming.

If you combine both of those strategies with relaxation efforts (conscious breathing, for example), your brain will begin to automatically put all of the elements together. This is real-world brain training.

Many great athletes use the power of rituals to help them train their brains and their bodies. I recently asked my friend Justin Rose, a golfer currently on the PGA Tour, if there were any pre-shot rituals he used to help him focus on the upcoming shot. "First thing I do, to start any routine, is take a deep breath. That gets me in the moment and makes anything I tell myself more meaningful," he said. The focus phrase Justin uses? "Feel the swing at target," he says. "This helps me commit to the shot rather than worry about the outcome."

The Power of the Checklist

The other day I was getting ready to board a plane in snowy Salt Lake City when I happened to peek outside and notice the pilot doing his checks on the outside of the plane. It was absolutely freezing, snow heavily falling, but the pilot had a step-by-step process that had to be followed before we could board. As someone who is a very nervous flyer, this helped me calm down a bit as it reassured me that there was a thorough process in place to help keep me safe.

When I asked my friend George Dom (former Navy air wing commander and Blue Angels flight leader) if he had some sort of image or phrase he focused on to perform at an incredibly high level on a daily basis, he told me that there was never just one thing. Instead he used a series of pre-flight rituals and checklists to ensure all considerations were made and all relevant information was communicated. He described this process as "entering a preflight bubble".

> "The briefing room was as quiet as possible to minimize distractions, and only those participating in the mission were allowed to attend. Entering the briefing room – always a few minutes early, NEVER late – you began the process of leaving the outside world behind and beginning to draw your mind to the present. To get in synch mentally with your wingmen, and to resolve any ambiguity about the mission objectives, the plan of actions, and how we would handle 'what if?' contingencies. As we commenced the briefing, the focus and attention of everyone involved came together. Anyone who appeared disengaged stood out like a sore thumb and would be called-out on it. No compromise in having everyone's full engagement – the stakes were too high."

141

He went on to describe visualization exercises, stepping through each phase of the mission with graphics to enhance understanding. "No multitasking, no checking paperwork before heading to the jets. We would don our flight gear and head to the flight deck or show line without delay in order to keep our focus."

Use a Training Log

In the spirit of keeping focused, here's a general suggestion: As you are developing your own list of steps for gaining and maintaining maximum mental fitness, you'll find that keeping a training log is an essential part of your program. Write down the most important strategies and exercises you want to focus on for a specific period of time and track your progress.

As time goes by and you develop a new mental habit, the strategies on your training log will become automatic so that you don't have to continue to write them down. Instead you can focus on building new supportive habits.

The type of training log makes no difference. You can write it by hand, create an Excel spreadsheet, or use an online tool. The important thing is that you keep it at the front of your mind and create specific rituals around how and when you will use it.

For example, I start every day by looking at my training log to remind me of what I'm working on in my life, before I look at what I need to work on for my job. Currently my focus is on having more fun and being more connected in my relationships, so checking in first thing gives me a chance to think through my plan for the day. What opportunities might come up to allow me to work on my goal, and how will I maximize them?

At the end of the day I look at my training log once again to check off whether or not I have accomplished what I set out to do. On some items a simple check mark tells me that I was able to do what I wanted, and for other items I score myself on a scale of 1–5, depending on how I did. Take my vitamins – check. Practice distraction resistance – 3.5.

This ritual of checking in and out during the day has been tough to implement, so I continue to research ways to make it easier. Some ideas I'm trying: putting the training log in a certain spot that I always look at (by the coffee pot), putting it on top of my to-do list when I prepare the night before, or setting it in front of the door so I literally have to walk over it in order to leave at the end of the day.

As I continue to practice, I find myself being more automatically driven to use the training log, a sign that I am creating a new habit. Although it may seem simplistic, it has become clear to me that clients who use a tracking system are always more successful at accomplishing their goals. By keeping a log they keep their goals and strategies top of mind, even if they have to adapt them along the way. For more information and to download the training log, visit the website at www.synerygprograms.com/sharptools.

Practice Mindfulness

Your focused attention is a present moment happening, right? And when your mind wanders and you're lost in thought in the past or the future, you temporarily lose your footing in here and now. Being able to maintain focused attention is very important at work and anywhere, so it's a good idea to spend some time each day training to be more present.

Psychologists estimate that most of us spend only about 10% of our time in the current moment. We spend about 50% of our time anticipating what's ahead of us and 40% reflecting on what's behind us.

Planning ahead and reflecting on the past is a vital part of life. But strengthening your ability to quickly and completely shift back into the present moment determines your mental power to bring focus to the action at hand. This is called cognitive shifting, and regular practice in this mental process is also called mindfulness meditation.

Because mindfulness meditation has received a lot of media coverage in the last few years, most people understand its health and performance benefits. The meditation practice can be incorporated into a brain-fitness routine, and is quite similar to what I've been teaching you already. Simply pause for a few minutes (or longer if you wish), watch your breathing, and at the same time, watch the thoughts that come flowing through your mind. By distancing yourself from your thoughts and becoming non-attached to them (i.e., not reacting or going off into associated thinking), you enter into a state of inner peace and clarity, which you can then bring back with you when you re-enter your work routine.

Even with full awareness of its benefits, most people still struggle with incorporating the practice into their busy schedule, which is why I asked my friend Kelley McCabe, former Wall Street broker and founder of eMindful, to provide some insight as to how a busy professional can incorporate these strategies into an already jam-packed day.

"Take shorter periods of time," she said. "When you wake up in the morning and don't have a lot of time to sit and be mindful, set a goal: Take 100 breaths, trying to be mindful of the sensations involved with breathing. (If 100 sounds daunting, as it did to me, start with 10 and gradually increase as you practice.) If you get distracted, don't judge. Just come right back and focus again on your breath."

Formal training is not required for mastering mindfulness breaks, although just like lifting weights, proper technique will help maximize your results. Here are some guidelines, which also apply to the other exercises I'm teaching you:

Principles of mindfulness:

1. Non-judgment: become an impartial witness to your own experience – just observe without reacting.

2. Patience: allow your experiences to unfold in their own time; don't expect anything at all – just 'be' with yourself.

3. Beginner's mind: entertain a willingness to see everything as if for the first time; each new moment is, after all, unique and new.

4. Trust: have faith in your own intuition and authority, and enjoy the pure experience of just being your authentic self.

5. Non-striving: have no goal other than sitting quietly, watching your breaths come and go, and watching your thoughts come and go – just 'be' without doing or expecting anything at all.

6. Acceptance: embrace all things and experiences as they actually are in the present moment, without needing anything to change.

7. Non-censoring: allow your inner experiences and thoughts to come and go with complete freedom without engaging with them at all.

One of the greatest techniques you can exercise and master is the ability to shift quickly into a state of mindfulness whenever you want to – to be purely here in the present moment, not judging, not engaged in the ongoing drama around you.

Biofeedback is an excellent tool to assist with practicing mindfulness, as it provides immediate feedback on your ability to navigate your thoughts and emotions. It can also help busy professionals become centered because it gives you something specific to focus on, and watching the monitors change can be fun and game-like, especially for those who are more analytical in nature. (For more on biofeedback, check out www.HeartMath.org.)

Take short breaks into mindfulness awareness throughout your day, and you brighten not only your own mind and inner experience, but also the energy you exude to the world around you. Throughout this book, you're strengthening your ability to do this.

Play Games For Mental Strength

In just the opposite direction of mindfulness, playing games can also strengthen your mind. We just saw how meditation makes you feel better and sharpens your brain through temporarily disengaging with the world around you. Playing games exercises the performance function of the mind by stimulating thinking and thus creating new pathways in the brain, or expanding existing ones.

Playing a game also temporarily removes you from all the stressful engagements that otherwise dominate your mind. Having fun using your brain maximizes the healthy stimulation of mental performance.

What kind of games? As long as you have to think in order to play, then games and puzzles can stimulate brain strength. Of course, if you've played a particular game for years and years, the benefit will be decreased because you start to play with your 'auto-brain.' Make sure the games or puzzles follow the three key components of successful brain training:

- specific – targeting a mental ability you want to target, and that has real-world applications

- challenging – causing you to actually think

- repetitive – just like exercise, being practiced regularly to continue to provide a benefit

Computer games can exercise your brain, yes. Those that are interactive also add interpersonal dimensions. And of course, games you play in person with someone or a circle of friends are best because they include the key component of expanding your experience of social connection.

So decide to build into your weekly schedule, on a firm basis, at least one time when you take an hour or two to play a game. Also, see if you can include an athletic game in your schedule, which provides you with a physical and mental energy boost in addition to cross training physical and mental coordination and flexibility!

Top Techniques for Training Mental Strength

In review, and to get you thinking a bit more about how you might create your own strength training strategy, here is a list of key actions you can take regularly, to bring more clarity and focused attention to your life:

1) Distraction Resistance

Avoid big distractions by turning them off. A client once told me that when his team goes into meetings they use the "boarding door has been closed" rule, requiring anything with an on/off switch to be turned off. Not on silent mode or vibrate, but off. Even the faint sound of a phone vibrating can have anyone within hearing distance wondering who might be calling and what phone calls he or she may be missing.

Some common mental energy drainers include cell phone/ Blackberry/iPhone, computer monitor, background noise, bad lighting, and uncomfortable chairs.

Remember – turn it off or tune it out.

- What are your top mental drainers?

- What distractions can you turn off?

- What distractions do you need to practice tuning out?

2) Mental Rehearsal

Just thinking about what you want to do can build strength in the areas of the brain that support that behavior.

In a study by neuroscience pioneer Alvaro Pascual-Leone, two groups of people who had never studied piano were given a series of notes to play and told which fingers to move to hit specific keys. One group sat in front of a keyboard for two hours a day for five days, imagining playing the piano and hearing the correct tones. The other group actually practiced playing the piano for the same amount of time.

Brain scans were done before, during, and after the experiment, and a computer was used to measure the accuracy of the performances. By the end of the study, brain change and accuracy were the same in both groups[11]. (Note: thinking about going to the gym is not the same as working out!)

What is something you'd like to improve upon, and how might you use mental rehearsal to become better prepared? Keep in mind, this works for both business and personal life. A great way to prepare to be fully engaged with family or friends at the end of the day is to actually visualize yourself spending time with them, able to pay full attention, with extraordinary energy and focus.

3) Use a Training Log

A training log is an essential part of any training program. Writing down specific steps for your plan works as a reminder and a place to track progress.

Over time, steps on your training log will become automatic so that you don't have to continue to write them down, and instead you can focus on building new habits.

Remember, the type of training log makes no difference. You can write it by hand, create an Excel spreadsheet, or use an online tool. The important thing is that you keep it at the front of your mind and create specific rituals around how and when you will use it.

Some ideas to help consistency: put the training log in a certain spot that you always look at (coffee pot, refrigerator, taped to your computer monitor), put it on top of your to-do list when you prepare the night before, or set it in front of the door so you literally have to walk over it to enter your office in the morning and/or leave at the end of the day.

As you continue to practice, you will find yourself being more automatically driven to use the training log, a sign that you are creating a new habit.

Weekly Training Log							
30-day *SHARP* Challenge Focus: Boost clarity and creativity at work and at home							
This week's goal: Reduce stress and feelings of overload by incorporating more recovery							
SHARP Strategies for this week:	Monday	Tuesday	Wednesday	Thursday	Friday	Saturday	Sunday
60 minutes of physical activity daily	X	X	X		X	X	X
Recharge break 3x/day (11, 2, 5)	X		X	X			
Check in with accountability partner daily via video email	X	X	X	X	X		
Other supportive rituals already established:							
Cardio minimum 3x/week	X	X	X		X	X	X
Weekly massage				X			
Mindful engagement with clients	4	4	3.5	5	n/a		

Download a copy of the SHARP Training Log at
www.synergyprograms.com/sharptools

4) Chunk Your Day

Time management is an important strategy when it comes to getting things done, but it's not just time that we need to manage. The mental energy that we give to the time that we have determines how productive that time will be. To avoid multitasking, chunk your day into time blocks so that you can focus more specifically and purposefully during that time frame.

The length of time can vary, as long as you have a plan ahead of time and schedule movement breaks at least every 90 minutes to keep your focus. Breaking big projects down (chunking) into smaller steps can also help you avoid getting distracted by the big picture or feeling overwhelmed.

Keep in mind that time blocks may need to get shorter as the day goes on to help manage energy and maintain focus as your energy levels are naturally declining a bit.

Sample day

8:00–8:50	Plan for the day – organize tasks by priority
8:50–9:00	Walk to Starbucks for coffee
9:00–10:30	Priority #1 task(s)
10:30–10:45	Recharge Break (or stretching, light exercise)
10:45–12:00	E-mail
12:00–12:45	Lunch away from desk/office
12:45–1:30	Priority #2 task(s)
1:30–1:45	Recharge Break (or yoga, meditation)
1:45–3:00	Priority #3 task(s)

3:00–3:15	Afternoon snack, walk stairs for 10 minutes
3:15–4:15	Priority #4 task(s)
4:15–4:30	Recharge Break (or call a friend, laugh)
4:30–5:30	Priority #5 task(s), and/or wrap up for day

5) 5-minute Laser Focus

Each day, choose a project or task that you've been putting off for some reason. Set a timer for five minutes, go to work with total focus, and get as much of that task done as you can without allowing any disruptions at all. Train single-mindedness!

For example, the "5-Minute Room Rescue," proposed by home organizer Marla Cilley, recommends you go to the worst room in your house and as the timer ticks down, you go to work getting things organized. When the timer alarm sounds, you can stop organizing, knowing you made some progress.[12]

Sit at your desk, run your 5-minute timer, and identify something that begs your attention. Go to work on this, and entirely disregard any external disruption for the entire five minutes (unless there truly is an emergency you need to deal with).

SHARP Sprints

Here are some specific activities that you can do in a short time-frame to increase mental focus:

2-minute Laser Focus

When you don't have five minutes to give, try the laser focus exercise for a shorter timeframe to continue to practice your ability to give your attention to one thing at a time. Set a timer with an alarm to let you know when two minutes is up, and you'll know you made some progress, even if the task isn't quite finished.

Challenge Yourself

Think of something you usually do on automatic pilot, and instead do it differently. These mental and physical changes will challenge and stimulate your brain, and wake you up to the present moment.

For example, a) for one meal a day, eat with your non-dominant hand; b) drive a different route to work; c) shop at a different grocery store; or d) listen to the phone with the other ear.

Each morning, spend a few moments thinking through what you do during the day without much conscious awareness, choose one of these, and mix it up somehow so that you do it in a different way.

Move It, Move It!

Physical activity is one of the best ways to promote the strength and development of your brain. Set your timer for one minute, and do a quick exercise to get your heart pumping, boost brain chemicals, and circulate oxygen and glucose to your brain.

Stretching, jumping jacks, squats, lunges, pushups, dips – it doesn't matter which in particular, just make sure you regularly move.

If you have more time, you can spend another minute or two switching up the exercises.

Count Down, Count Up

As mentioned before, counting exercises (especially when matched with breathing) are simple yet powerful. Choose a counting exercise such as starting at 100 and counting down by 5s, and when you get good at this, by 7s.

This is a common assessment done to test concentration, focus, and attention – what memory specialists now call 'registration.' You can make up any counting pattern that you want, moving in any direction, as long as you feel that you are challenged to think.

Red Dot Experience

To help exercise your mental awareness of the present moment visually, place a few red dot stickers around your workplace or home, in places that you will easily see during the day. Each time you see a red dot, commit to increasing your mindfulness by bringing your attention to the here and now. Tune into your breathing, to the emotions you are feeling, and your whole-body presence in the moment. Shift cognitively from being lost in thought, to focusing on your sense of awareness.

Training Take Away

What we **don't pay attention to is just as important as what we do pay attention to**, and being distracted by the wrong things can decrease our performance. While you might not be leading the Blue Angels in flight, when it comes to being extraordinary at what's most important to you – parent, partner, friend, leader, advisor – the stakes are always high. Training our brain to be more **focused** is **strength training** for the brain, which allows us to bring our best mental energy to the present moment.

CHAPTER 10
Flexibility Training – Developing Resilience

A flexible brain allows us to apply mental energy toward doing things that move us in directions we want to go. Our natural tendency is to get stuck in habitual patterns and to function automatically in survival mode. But this low-awareness approach to life often overrides any sense of purposeful direction or flexibility in choices and outcomes. Rather than just going with the preconditioned flow of habits, a flexible brain is able to learn, evaluate, and adapt as needed, changing our mindset consciously to focus on what is most important to us.

To see a video of author Heidi Hanna talking about positivity training for mental flexibility, scan the QR code below

This ability of being able to adjust our perspective to see things in new, more positive ways impacts not only our happiness, but also improves our performance and resilience.

For instance, when it comes to cognitive health and fitness, our ability to age successfully may have more to do with our attitude than any other factor. According to a study by Becca Levy and her colleagues at Yale, having a positive attitude made far more difference than lowering blood pressure or reducing cholesterol in overall health in the elderly, providing more benefits than exercise, maintaining a healthy weight, and not smoking. Based on the responses of more than 650 people, **those who had a positive view of aging lived an average of 7.5 years longer than those who were negative about it.**[1]

In her book *Counterclockwise*, Ellyn Langer describes mental flexibility as a critical element of healthy living.[2] "I've discovered a very important truth about human psychology: Certainty is a cruel mindset. It hardens our minds against possibility, and closes us off from the world we actually live in."

Training ourselves to be more flexible in our attitudes allows us to stay open-minded; to think outside the box, boost our creativity, and build overall resilience in life.

The Power of Perception

"We don't see things as they are, we see them as we are."

Anaïs Nin

It's not what happens to us that ultimately forms our memories and shapes our brain; it's how we experience and interpret what happens to us.

Unfortunately, many of us function in survival mode throughout the day, reacting to the world based on previous programming from our childhood, and we're not mindful of how our brains perceive and interpret what's happening around us. Thus, we remain locked into old behaviors and attitudes that are often negative and self-defeating.

When you increase your present moment awareness of how you process the world, as we're exploring in this book, you can naturally develop a more positive and growth-oriented perspective, which can in turn have an uplifting impact on how you respond both physically and psychologically.

You have a unique perspective that you carry around with you and apply to everything you experience, thus coloring your reaction or response. You either react negatively or respond positively, depending on how you interpret the situation.

Perspective is manifested in many ways through your thoughts and emotions. As you combine all the various messages you tell yourself about what you're experiencing throughout the day, you continue to develop your 'life story.' Over time, these bits and pieces of your story create and define your mindset. You see yourself and the world around you in certain ways because you react or respond in particular patterns.

In order to have a positive perspective that will support a flexible brain, it's critical to develop a life story that supports and augments a positive, growth-oriented mindset.

The Significance of Story

As Dr. Loehr discusses in his book *The Power of Story*, "**The most important story we will ever tell is the story we tell to ourselves about ourselves.**"[3] Each of us carries around in the back of our mind a story that explains who we are and why we do what we do. Our story is our internal narrative. And all the private comments we make to ourselves either move us forward in the direction that is most important to us, or block us from getting where we want to go.

This internal dialogue can move us toward our goals, or pull us off course, and is often the most powerful predictor of positive change.

Our perceptions, emotions, and relationships are all closely shaped by how we choose to tell our story. As studies show, we don't remember things exactly, but instead we create a story that represents our interpretation or relationship to that event; so even our memory is a narrative-driven process. Everything we keep as a memory has a story connected to it, whether it be an object, a relationship, or an experience.

Luckily, how we choose to store that information is not necessarily set in stone. In fact, over time, our memories can be reframed and rewritten to optimally support our current state of mind, or the state of mind we want to be in. As Michael Margolis states in *Believe Me*, "Something once traumatic can eventually be transformed into a growth experience, or equally remain as a tragedy that forever changed one's life for the worst."[4]

In your own life, if you look honestly at yourself, would you say that you're an optimistic person, or pessimistic? Do you tend to expect the worst to happen, or the best? Do you have a low sense of self-esteem, or a high self-esteem? Do you usually spend your time focused on bad things that have happened in the past, and worrying about bad things that might happen in the future, or are you usually thinking about hopeful things that raise your spirit?

We all live in a world that seems focused on the negative, which is obvious from watching just ten minutes of the nightly news. Unfortunately our 'reptilian' and 'monkey brains' are programmed to focus on danger or potential danger, and so we're easily seduced into fixating on the negative things around us.

But, you do have the choice to take charge of your mind's focus, and develop the power and flexibility to refocus your attention in positive directions that don't drag you down.

The result? When you start to hold your focus purposefully on the positive rather than the negative, your entire inner story naturally changes – you start seeing your life as more hopeful, enjoyable, and fulfilling.

By exercising your brain to shift in directions that boost your vitality, health, performance, and pleasure in life.

Mindset Matters

Your mindset is the overarching theme of your life story, the lens through which you look at life. In her book, *Mindset: The New Psychology of Success*, Carol Dweck of Stanford University states that a person's mindset is based on their beliefs about their most basic qualities and abilities.[5] Dweck separates mindset types into two fundamental categories: a fixed mindset and a growth mindset.

Fixed Mindset: Someone who believes that intelligence and talent are primarily genetically based fixed traits – either you have it or you don't – is considered to be of a fixed mindset. These individuals tend to believe that success is based primarily on talent, and may be quick to dismiss effort and hard work as being for the weak or less intelligent.[5]

People with a fixed mindset often opt for easier tasks that require less effort, and they may give up quickly. Whether it's related to work or an important relationship, fixed-mindset people will often throw in the towel faster than people who believe they have the ability to work hard for change.

Growth Mindset: In this more positive mindset, it's assumed that we can train and work to improve our performance and our lives – that we're not stuck with just our genetic traits. Difficulties are seen as opportunities for growth. People with a growth mindset are more willing to take risks, put in extra effort, and recognize the benefits of learning, regardless of outcome.

In her research, Dweck finds that individuals trained to nurture a growth mindset more often pursue goals related to learning and not just performance. And they believe they can purposefully act to develop their brains, abilities, and talents.

Multiple studies show that a growth mindset is beneficial in many ways for aiding business success:

1. Negotiators with a growth mindset were shown to be more able to push past obstacles and reach a mutually beneficial agreement.

2. Business school students who were taught a growth mindset learned more skills and received better grades in their negotiation class.

3. Leaders benefit from a growth mindset because they perceive the value of coaching and training their employees, and are quicker to reinforce improvement in their team than leaders with a fixed mindset.

Your mindset is all about where you focus your attention each new moment. Focus just where there are problems, and your life is full of problems. Focus on opportunities, and that's what you will see.

According to Fredrickson's "Broaden and Build" theory, positive emotions lead us to see the world around us with greater perspective.[6] They allow us to focus on things such as building relationships, collaborating with others, and thinking outside the box. Positive emotions broaden the scope of our attention and increase our ability to use different elements of our cognitive functioning. They widen the lens through which we see the world around us, enabling us to connect more dots, which enhances our ability to be creative.

These positive emotions flood our brains with endorphins that not only make us feel good, but also improve 'mental muscle.' Dopamine, for example, is released in the brain when we experience hope and pleasure, and experiments show that dopamine helps build stronger neural pathways.

Positive emotions also have a significant impact on our overall health and well-being. When we are happy, our immune system functions better, making us recover more quickly from injury or illness. A positive mindset improves resilience, reduces pain and inflammation, and decreases our risk of stroke.

You Have More Control Than You Think

The evidence is clear – people with a realistic positive outlook and a growth mindset in all ways outperform people caught up in negativity. Most of us at least sometimes find ourselves a bit stuck with negative thoughts and emotions. Fortunately, as we're seeing throughout this book, you can take charge and train your mind to think differently, and to see life through a more positive inner lens.

Multiple studies have shown that even by using simple techniques such as journaling, regularly listing things we're grateful for, and sending thank-you notes to others, we can train the brain to be more optimistic.

Positive psychology is not just about seeing life through rose-colored glasses. It's about facing reality honestly, and then choosing to focus in directions that best serve us – positive directions that encourage the feeling of happiness.

According to positive psychologist Sonja Lyubomirsky in her book, *The How of Happiness*, research suggests that up to 40% of our happiness stems from intentional activities (those we choose to engage in).[7] What's very surprising to most people is that **only about 10% has to do with life circumstances**.

Practicing positive focusing as part of cognitive fitness is based on exercises that build your brain's ability to focus on what's good and healthy in life, right here and now.

More than just putting you in a better mood, this type of 'mindset makeover' has been shown to significantly benefit performance in many aspects of life. Studies by Lyubomirsky and colleagues showed that positive affect fosters sociability, altruism, higher self-esteem, stronger immune systems, more effective conflict-resolution skills, and original thinking. [8]

Consider the placebo effect: When people think they're getting some sort of health benefit or medical treatment, they often feel better because their mind tells them they should feel better. And their physical condition often improves as well.

You have the power to change your story and your mindset by actively changing where you focus your attention. Over the next few days, begin to notice where you are focusing your attention. When you catch yourself dwelling on worries about the future, remorse about the past, negative judgments about people around you or about yourself, stop! Remember that you can focus elsewhere, and practice doing so.

And please keep in mind that change takes time. Improvement in fitness training comes step-by-step, moment-by-moment, and exercise-by-exercise. You have the ability to develop discipline in retraining your focus, and to establish a schedule for practicing the strategies that will move you in the direction you want to move, one step at a time.

At the end of this book we'll review all of the exercises being discussed here, so that if you choose to do so, you can create an exercise log for each week to help you stick with the commitment to brighten your mindset.

Corporate Mindset Ratings

Companies as a whole can be rated based on their 'positivity ratio,' and studies show that the higher the positivity in a company, the more likely that company is to thrive. It turns out that employees who are positive in their attitudes have many advantages over those who are negative or neutral, including mental flexibility.

According to Lyobomirsky, "People in a positive mood are more likely to have richer associations with existing knowledge structures (things we already have committed to memory), and thus are more likely to be more flexible and original.

Martin Seligman, often called the "Godfather" of positive psychology, claimed that positive people are more resilient because when difficulties strike they are able to perform better, and their physical health is stronger.[9]

Barbara Fredrickson has studied the power of positivity in companies that she has researched and consulted. Fredrickson and her team analyzed the words that are said in business meetings in order to determining their 'positivity ratio' or the ratio of positive to negative statements.

According to Fredrickson, companies with a positivity ratio higher than 2.9:1 (or 2.9 positive statements for every 1 negative statement) were clearly successful. Below that ratio, companies weren't doing well economically.[10]

Many of the exercises I'm recommending in this book for personal mindset improvement can also be taught and employed in companies as a whole. When employees realize that their employers actually want them to enjoy work more, and take time each day for self-nurturing such qualities as mindfulness, positive mindset, and so forth, employees will respond positively in kind.

Exercising Gratitude

One of the quickest ways to boost happiness and create a brighter mindset is to actively appreciate what you already have in your life. To accomplish this, positive psychologists and cognitive therapists alike recommend simple gratitude exercises that give you the opportunity to scan the world around you in order to see what is going well, and acknowledge it.

When done regularly, these exercises of gratitude, or thankfulness, help to train the brain to focus more on the good things in your life rather than the bad.

In a study on gratitude writing, participants who wrote down three good things each day for a week were happier at one, three, and six-month follow-ups than those who didn't.[11]

And expressing gratefulness has a holistic effect. According to multiple studies, people who actively write a daily gratitude list feel more optimistic, exercise more frequently, and report fewer physical complaints than people who don't. They also experience more positive emotions, fewer negative emotions, and exhibit more helpful behavior towards friends and neighbors.[12]

Please keep in mind that being optimistic and expressing gratitude doesn't mean being unrealistic. As we discussed earlier, a positive mindset is still able to see the challenges of reality, but it also enables you to see beyond just the difficulties – to see challenge as a growth opportunity instead of a roadblock.

Therefore, training your brain to see positive things more regularly, and to feel gratitude for those positive things, is a realistic activity that will help you create a more beneficial mindset and overall life experience.

Cultivating Creativity

Nurturing flexibility and an open-minded perspective is also important because it enables us to think outside the box. Creativity requires a healthy, expansive, playful imagination that negativity stifles. As children, most of us were encouraged to use our imagination regularly, dream big, and see life as a playful adventure. But somewhere along the way, we were told to be realistic – to grow up, get serious, and act like adults (how boring).

In the process, our inherent playful creativity became inhibited, all while picking up our parents' bad habit of worrying too much and focusing on the negative, which directly wilts creativity.

Keep in mind that creativity is not only an important trait to have in our personal life, it's critical for most business professionals. Creativity helps us stand out from the competition when it comes to promoting our business and ourselves. We can strengthen important client relationships by utilizing creativity to create what my friend John Evans, Executive Director at Janus Labs, calls 'Wow moments' – when a client is delighted by an act that is spontaneous, thoughtful, and meaningful to them personally.

Feeling creative allows us to be more open-minded and flexible. This enables us to see different perspectives and make more thoughtful decisions that incorporate the best of what the team brings to the table.

Boosting positive thinking increases our ability to be creative because it allows us to focus on what's going well, instead of becoming narrowly focused on what's going wrong. When you're in a bad mood, your tendency is to fall back on what you already know in a defensive manner, as opposed to gathering ideas and insight from other people, and weighing all of the options.

A quick way to boost creativity is to spend a few minutes exercising your mental flexibility through positivity training. Something as simple as writing down three things you're grateful for every morning can help train your brain to scan the world for positive things, instead of always focusing on the negative ones.

The activity that seems to create the greatest immediate benefit (the greatest boost in positivity) is writing a letter of thanks to someone you appreciate. If possible, read the letter aloud to that person. If that is not an option, you will still personally experience an increase in happiness just by expressing yourself, even if you're the only one who will ever read it.

Action Plan: Flexibility Training

You can train your brain to see life more positively by exercising your mental flexibility. When you discipline yourself each day to pause and write down a physical list of the positive things that happened during that day, your brain is purposefully forced to focus on and acknowledge positive interactions and events.

The more often you do this type of 'soul searching' the more your brain releases chemicals that make the positive connections stronger based on the 'use it or lose it' principle of brain plasticity.

Soon, focusing on the positive becomes your new automatic pilot mode. Because our brain can only focus on one thing at a time, paying attention to the positive leaves little energy to spend on the negative.

Meanwhile, a new focus habit is being formed and strengthened. Over time, that change gives you a more positive lens through which to view your life – and your story changes, for the better!

Top Techniques for Training Mental Flexibility

In review, and to get you thinking a bit more about how you might create your own flexibility training strategy, here is a list of key actions you can take regularly to become more flexible, creative, and joyous in your life:

1) Get Your Story Right

We all have negative stories and attitudes about ourselves, about life in general, and about people around us. From virtually birth onward, we were conditioned to have similar ways of thinking and acting as our parents, and most of us fail to consciously break free from attitudes and beliefs that don't seem to fit in our own lives.

According to cognitive scientists, at the core of our 'story' is a set of one-liner beliefs and assumptions that tend to strongly influence how we perceive life. For instance, if we were taught that we aren't inherently any good at sports when we were young, we'll continue to see ourselves this way unless we actively reject the attitude, and begin training our bodies for success in sports. Likewise, many people developed a negative attitude of their intellectual abilities, or even their basic self-worth.

You might also find that your story is a tale about life being unfair, or people generally being untrustworthy, or work being boring, or money being evil – the list of one-liner childhood attitudes that run our lives as adults is very long, and often highly detrimental to living a good life. It may be time to re-write your story.

Here's what you can do: each day, commit to spending five minutes looking at your negative assumptions. Identify them, evaluate them consciously, and then choose to begin reinforcing the opposite of the negative belief.

For instance, if you find that deep down you somehow believe that you're not creative or intelligent, not attractive or interesting, not strong or successful. Whatever it is, write out the opposite, positive statement, and reflect on it throughout the day. Repeating these types of phrases will not just make you feel better in the moment; the process will actually rewire your mental patterns so that over time your thoughts and beliefs will be more naturally supportive.

Say to yourself over and over, "I am creative and intelligent," or perhaps "I am interesting and attractive," or "I am strong and successful." These focusing statements will aim your intent in the direction you want to move.

Step by step, as weeks go by and you continue to discipline your mind to entertain these positive thoughts about yourself, your story will change, your attitudes will expand and shift, and your life will improve. But to get results, you must exercise your mind by regularly training a new way of thinking.

2) Practice Gratitude

Each morning, take a moment to reflect and write down three things for which you're grateful. Or if you'd prefer to experience thankfulness in the evenings before bed, try counting your blessings. List or journal about what went well today. For an even greater positivity boost, exchange blessings lists with your partner or spouse.

Try this right now to experience a boost in happiness: What are three things for which you are grateful?

1.

2.

3.

You may want to also start a 'blessings journal,' in which you keep track of all your gratitude lists in one place, so you can have the opportunity to go back through them when you aren't feeling quite as grateful.

We all have times when we experience the blues, or find ourselves in a funk, so having a journal to remind us of what matters most and the many blessings we have in our life can help boost our sense of gratitude during difficult times.

As I mentioned earlier, another way to practice gratitude is to write a gratitude letter. Think of someone who has contributed to your well-being and whom you've never fully thanked. Write a letter or e-mail to that person describing the benefits you have received. Be detailed. Describe how the actions made you feel. Take this letter and perhaps read it aloud to that person. If possible, do this face to face so you can share the moment together.

3) Make-over Your Mindset

As we discussed, you can create a new, more expansive and positive mindset by learning to actively focus on positive things, which opens your mind up to entertain different ways of thinking.

Writing is a good way to get a better sense of your current mindset and to make adjustments so that you can see things from a new perspective. Here's a basic exercise that you can expand each day:

Think of and write down a negative attitude, statement, judgment, belief, or assumption that seems to sometimes dominate your mind, perhaps one like this:

"Things are falling apart – it's hopeless."

If this attitude tends to be stuck in the back of your mind, it will pollute your whole day, dragging down your mood and taking away your power to effect positive change.

See what happens when you exercise your attitude muscle by saying the opposite to yourself, and holding this positive statement in your mind all day. It will transform your mindset, unleash positive power, and boost your mood.

"I am doing well in tough circumstances. I feel hopeful."

Each day in the morning, discipline yourself to come up with another negative statement that sometimes grabs at you. Write down the negative one-liner, and then reflect on the fact that the opposite can also be seen as true. Write that down, and hold this positive statement in the back of your mind throughout the day.

Then in the evening, write the positive statement again and write a paragraph or two about how holding the positive thought in your mind impacted your day. Consider your actions, your mood, your relating, your self-esteem, and your deeper sense of self.

4) Quiet Your Mind

Of all the mind-body practices, meditation takes the prize for the most research currently available to validate its benefits in multiple dimensions – body, mind, and spirit. There are many ways to use meditation techniques for mental flexibility. A focusing exercise is considered meditation if it:

- is a self-induced state

- utilizes a specific and clearly defined technique

- initiates relaxation somewhere during the process

- involves a quieting of thoughts in the mind

- incorporates a self-focus skill or 'anchor' for attention

Meditation as we're approaching it in this book involves pausing for a few minutes at a time (or more), and turning your focus of attention directly to the experience of your own breathing. This brings you into the present moment, quiets your mind, and wakes up a healthy whole-body awareness in the here and now. In this relaxed state, your body can regain its equilibrium, your mind can restore its inner balance, and your breathing can return to a natural flow. Stress dissolves, clarity emerges, and joy can be felt again.

Beyond that, there are no set rules for how or when to practice meditation. The key is that you schedule it into your day, and try to keep your practice consistent so that you can rely on the technique when you need it most.

I also want to mention that you don't even have to sit quietly to meditate. The Tibetans talk about "meditation in action" where you remember to be aware of your breathing and our whole-body presence, no matter what you're doing. There are also walking meditations that you can do every time you walk somewhere, even if it's just down the hallway.

As long as you're turning your mind's focus of attention purposefully to your breathing, and focusing fully on your presence in the current moment, you're in a meditative state, and will reap all the benefits we've discussed.

5) Motivate With Mantras

Positive mantras, similar to 'focus phrases', are another way to provide new inspiring language to the brain. The simpler the mantra, the easier it is to recall in challenging or stressful situations.

There are no rules for creating a mantra. The key is coming up with a phrase that is calming, inspiring, or motivating to you, that you can call on quickly without much effort, and that focuses your mental and emotional energy in a way that is best suited for the occasion.

Athletes often use mantras to "get their head in the game" before or during a competition. Individuals with high levels of stress or anxiety can find significant relief by practicing mantras. If coupled with deep breathing practice, a simple repeated phrase can stimulate the relaxation response, which helps the body balance out the negative stress response. (For more information on the relaxation response, see Dr. Herbert Benson's book *The Relaxation Revolution*.)

The use of positive mantras has been especially beneficial to me, both personally and professionally. I've found that the use of a positive phrase such as "light and easy" helps me to stay relaxed while running marathons. I also credit the use of mantras for helping me to control anxiety I have struggled with for most of my life related to public speaking and flying.

There are a lot of great ways you can use mantras during the day to help create the right story for yourself, increase resilience, and motivate you toward your goal. Mantras may be simple, but they are powerful if you can come up with a word or phrase that is positive and meaningful to you, and that you practice consistently.

Each time you repeat a mantra, your brain fires chemicals to help strengthen neural connections, making your new way of thinking more automatic.

Examples of Positive Mantras

- I am healthy and happy
- I have a lot of energy
- I study and comprehend fast
- My mind is calm
- I am able to relax in almost every situation
- My thoughts are under my control
- I radiate love and happiness
- I am surrounded by love
- I have a wonderful, satisfying job
- Things keep getting better

Now that you get the idea, please take time to write down some mantras of your own.

SHARP Sprints

The following are quick activities that increase mental flexibility:

Thank You or Just Because Note

Jot a quick note to a family member, friend, colleague, or even someone you just met, to show your appreciation or to simply let them know you're thinking of them.

Visualization

Think through something that you want to practice, and visualize in as much detail as possible what it would feel like, look like, and sound like. Use as many senses as you can to help provide a true-to-life mental experience.

Short Guided Imagery

It can be difficult to focus on relaxation when your mind is being pulled in a million different directions. Guided imagery provides step-by-step instructions for you to follow in order to reach a desired state of mind.

Look Back and Forth

Gratitude doesn't have to be just about what's already happened. Write down some things you are grateful for that occurred in the past, and then fast forward, just a little bit, and write down what you're looking forward to.

Rewrite a Short Story

When dealing with a challenging situation, quickly write down bullet points that are negative and see if you can reframe them in a more positive way. Recall a time one door closed but another one opened.

Training Take Away

What we **perceive is what we experience**, and focusing in a different direction can completely change what we see ... literally. As the great psychologist William James once said, "My experience is what I agree to attend to." Developing a **positive, growth-oriented, opportunity-based mindset** is **flexibility training** for the brain. This will allow us to be resilient in complex situations, and to see the positive in even the most challenging of circumstances.

CHAPTER 11
Endurance Training – Healthy Aging

Having endurance means being able to sustain the wear and tear of the daily grind throughout your lifetime. By utilizing the cognitive fitness training program outlined in this book, you can learn to shift your auto-brain away from habitual and reflexive survival mode toward a new way of thinking and behaving that moves you in the direction of your long-term goals.

Along with knowing all the various aspects of cognitive fitness, it's vital to develop a realistic program that you can stick with for the long run.

Most importantly, if you want to train your brain to work more efficiently and to age successfully, you must be as consistent as possible. As you incorporate new supportive habits into your life, it's important to practice repetition with long-term devotion, so that your daily exercises become mostly automated and thus require less energy.

To reap the best results, endurance training needs to include both regular training and also regular rest periods where you periodically give yourself a break from doing any work.

181

The key is determining the ideal work/rest ratio that feels optimal for you – when you continue to feel challenged and stimulated, but also are able to relax and rest. Have you ever noticed that taking a day off from working out feels great, and two feels like a luxury, but after three it's very hard to start again?

Vladimir Horowitz, a famous pianist who performed well into his eighties, said this about consistency, "When I miss one day I notice. When I miss two days my wife notices. When I miss three days the world notices."[1]

So once a week or so, take a day off. Once a month perhaps, take two days away from your brain training. But try to maintain consistency as much as possible, and avoid letting yourself fall back into old patterns of forgetting to maintain your brain.

We Are All Aging – Let's Deal With It

Scientists tell us that even in our twenties, our brains are beginning to slow down and lose their edge a bit. And in our forties and fifties, if we don't stay in shape mentally, we definitely see a drop in cognitive performance and resilience. The program we're developing in this book will enable you to keep your brain in shape for the rest of your life – if you're consistent with your training routine.

Having a resilient brain allows you to enjoy successful, healthy aging. And with the right regimen in place, your brain health and cognitive fitness efforts may even prevent age-related disease and dementia. In anti-aging research it's widely accepted that, in order to age well, the structure of the neurons and their connections in the brain must remain strong and healthy, and that we must maintain a flexible mindset in order to decrease the negative impact of stress, maximize the benefits of positivity, and keep our memory sharp.

Maintaining and Training Memory

If you've ever forgotten something important, and wondered if you might be losing your mind, you are not alone. Even at a young age, most of us experience some forgetfulness. A weak memory can be provoked by poor nutrition (too much junk food) or even a lack of movement (sitting for too long). Oftentimes, temporary memory loss or mental fogginess can be caused by lack of sleep, emotional upsets, alcohol consumption, or medication. It can also be circumstantial, based on an overload of work or too many distractions.

However, noticeable memory loss for longer periods can also be a sign of weak brain strength, or low flexibility, which is why endurance training requires a combination of both.

Memory loss, especially in later life, can also be a symptom of brain disease, and although the research is still limited, experts agree that brain-training exercises have the potential to decrease the risk of developing Alzheimer's or other forms of dementia.[2]

Keep in mind what I mentioned earlier in the strength training section: A stronger, more flexible brain may mean that someone with plaques and tangles from Alzheimer's disease will never experience a single symptom.

As I researched memory for this book, I quickly realized that there was a lot more to maintaining memory than I initially thought. My association with memory up to this point had been all about healthy aging, based on my personal focus on learning more about preventing Alzheimer's due to my family history.

However, memory is not something we just want to maintain at our current levels. It's something that we can actively train to improve immediately. And for most of us, we probably should.

For instance, in any business it's important to stand out from the competition, and often the best way to do that is based on the relationship you create with your clients – a relationship that is deepened by remembering details about their lives.

I witnessed firsthand how a strong memory can benefit the development of new relationships when I worked at my previous job. My colleague, Chris Jordan, would always begin his lecture on exercise by asking the clients to turn over their nametags. He then would go around the room and state each person's first name, often with groups of up to 40 people at a time. Chris not only remembered their names the first day, but he continued to call them by name in the gym on days two and three, when they were no longer wearing name tags. He also was able to commit to memory the target heart rate zone for each individual.

Comments from clients who trained with Chris would almost always mention the fact that even in a group, he made them feel like an individual. This made them feel special and valuable, and made Chris a fantastic trainer who could quickly connect with his clients.

Research has suggested that less than 50 percent of our memory and brain function is inherited, which leaves a lot of room for us to control how our brain ages.

A growing number of experts believe that lifestyle-related issues such as obesity, diabetes, hypertension, smoking, sedentary lifestyle, high cholesterol, and chronic stress have the potential to increase the risk of developing cognitive impairment as much as 16-fold; a far greater risk than having a parent with Alzheimer's disease.[3]

We have a great ability to take charge of our own minds and change old patterns for the better. While my own memory is still a work in progress, I have noticed a definite improvement since I began working out my brain. And there are a few other things I've been able to do in my life that I never imagined I would do. The fact that I've been able to overcome my fears of flying and public speaking has allowed me to follow a career path I never dreamed possible – something I never could have done without making a conscious effort to retrain my brain.

Mind Over Matter – The Power Of Purpose

When our cognitive training is fueled by our deeper sense of purpose, there are few limitations to what we can accomplish.

I'd like to share a story from my client, David, a family-wealth director in Winter Park, Florida, who has used this type of real-world brain training to accomplish things he (and his doctors) never thought possible.

"I suffered a potentially life threatening accident over 25 years ago, which left me with an artificial hip, thirteen pins, and a metal plate. They thought I might be a paraplegic, then thought I might never walk again ... I still remember the first day when I could get up in the hospital and make it to the door of my hospital room. In the corridor I encountered a young grandchild walking along with his grandmother. The boy said, 'Look, Granny, that man has a walker just like you!' I admit I thought bad thoughts about that kid, but I also woke up to the feeling of determination to move beyond my walker.

I then had the opportunity to go through a one-on-one program with Dr. Loehr, and it was like a light bulb being turned on. He helped me to understand the meaning of full engagement with my purpose, and how determination and balance in all things in life is the key. Part of that balance issue is what you talk about in your book, Heidi, for upgrading your life's personal operating system. Doing some of your training and having the opportunity to better understand how my body works, and how important regaining balance is, has helped me tremendously in my personal and professional career.

As much as your *SHARP* Strategies are vital to boost your brainpower and excel in your chosen life, they can also be a key to discovering powers within yourself to push you to succeed. I just ran my third Boston Marathon three weeks ago with all of my pins, plates, clips, fusions, etc. **The brain is a power tool that, if trained properly, can 'will you' to accomplish pretty much anything** – and also to understand what's really important in life."

A sense of purpose beyond merely survival is at the core of what makes us human. We function best when we are on a mission that

186

truly matters, and when we're doing something that we believe in, we are always more on our game.

As he describes in one of my favorite books, *The Power of Purpose,* Robert Leider sought out to discover what people would do differently if they had the chance to 'do it all over again'.[4] The book was developed by interviewing adults over age 65 concerning some of the most important questions in life. The people interviewed consistently said that if they could live their lives over again, they would want to:

- **Be more reflective**

- **Be more courageous**

- **Be clear earlier about purpose**

There is nothing in those statements about spending more time in the office, making more money, being more famous, having more power, or any of the things that younger people often strive for. Purpose at deeper levels is the driving force behind everything we do, and with the right sense of purpose, unique to each individual, we can accomplish things that we never dreamed possible. Maybe more importantly, we can accomplish those things and feel proud of what we've done, knowing that it was done on purpose.

If I Had My Life to Live Over
by Nadine Stair (at age 85)

I'd dare to make more mistakes next time.
I'd relax. I would limber up.
I would be sillier than I have been this trip.
I would take fewer things seriously.
I would take more chances.

I would climb more mountains and swim more rivers.
I would eat more ice cream and less beans.
I would perhaps have more actual troubles
but I'd have fewer imaginary ones.

You see, I'm one of those people who live
sensibly and sanely hour after hour,
day after day.

Oh, I've had my moments,
and if I had it to do over again,
I'd have more of them.
In fact, I'd try to have nothing else.
Just moments, one after another,
instead of living so many years ahead of each day.

I've been one of those people who never go anywhere
without a thermometer, a hot water bottle, a raincoat
and a parachute.
If I had to do it again, I would travel lighter than I have.

If I had my life to live over,
I would start barefoot earlier in the spring
and stay that way later in the fall.
I would go to more dances.
I would ride more merry-go-rounds.
I would pick more daisies.

When purpose is discussed in the office, it's usually through some sort of corporate mission or vision statement. Yet, for the individual worker, there is often a disconnect between what is important to them personally and what the organization claims to stand for. Leider suggests that, "The failure of many organizations to enlist people in some kind of unselfish, non-quantitative purpose is at the root of many productivity problems today. **When we ignore purpose at work, we inhibit the highest motivator.**"

Purpose is also what drives our day-to-day behaviors, whether we realize it or not. Each day we are forced to answer the question, "Why do I get up in the morning?"

It is important to face this challenge of identifying our purpose on a regular basis in order to make sure that we are living in a way that is in harmony with our deepest values and beliefs.

Hopefully, your sense of your own purpose has been advancing while reading this book. For instance, we've been focusing on the extremely important purpose of choosing to live more in the moment rather than being lost in thought or memory too much of the time.

All of us, of course, go through times when we feel lost and lacking in direction. Purpose is not something we decide once and forget. It is important to make connecting to a purpose a part of our daily routine by building habits that make us take a look at what matters most on a regular basis.

You might consider trying one or more of the following:

1. Write your mission statement or personal vision on a Post-it note and put it on your mirror

2. Use a photo of people you care about as your screensaver

3. Play a song that inspires you at a strategic time of the day (or even make it your ringtone, as I did, so you hear it regularly)

Keep in mind that not only does purpose fuel our behavior, but living life on purpose may also help us live longer.

According to a study by Dr. Robert Butler and colleagues, individuals who have clear goals and believe they are making a difference with their life live longer and are sharper than those who do not.[5]

Maximize Results with Cross-Training

One way to fuse brain health and brain training together is to 'cross train' different aspects of both mental and physical fitness within the same activity. This gives you a greater return on your time and energy investment. Examples include laughter, massage, yoga, and walking.

Laugh Out Loud: Laughter is such great medicine that laughter therapy, groups, and clubs have sprouted out all over the country to help people improve their health and happiness. It's a bit sad to think that we may have to designate specific time for laughing, but just like everything else we've talked about so far, if you don't plan it, it's not likely to happen. Yes, we may laugh during the day from time to time, but because we are so busy, most of us hardly slow down long enough to allow ourselves to have a good belly laugh.

Laughter is beneficial in multiple ways. Physically, laughter stimulates most of the same endorphins (brain chemicals) as exercise and can increase blood flow and energy production.

Mentally, laughter helps us to get a nice break from stress and stimulates the relaxation response inside our body and mind.

In the 18th century Sebastian Chamfort wrote that "The most wasted day is one in which we have not laughed." And the famous editor and writer Norman Cousins explained in his best seller *Anatomy of an Illness* that laughter helped him overcome the pain of his severely debilitating disease of the endocrine system.[6]

"I made the joyous discovery that ten minutes of genuine belly laughter had an anesthetic effect and would give me at least two hours of pain-free sleep." Part of the therapy he designed for himself included watching Marx Brothers movies and reading humor books.

© Randy Glasbergen.
www.glasbergen.com

"Many people believe that laughter is the best medicine, so the government has declared a ban on all laughing until further studies can be done."

Get a Massage: If you've had a massage before, you're already aware of the immediate relaxation benefits, but you might not realize just how impactful regular massage can be on your physical and mental health. Several studies have demonstrated the ability for massage to decrease stress hormones and boost feel-good endorphins in the brain. Even just 15 minutes can have impressive results. According to a study published in the *International Journal of Neuroscience*, when compared to a control group that was asked to sit and relax for 15 minutes, the group who received massage showed significant decreases in cortisol and increases in serotonin and dopamine. The massage group also showed increased speed and accuracy when computing math problems[7].

Massage doesn't have to take place at a fancy resort spa (although it is a nice option). Memberships at clubs such as Massage Envy are inexpensive, especially when you consider the return you get on that investment: increased energy, improved performance, and decreased stress hormones. An increase in positive endorphins boosts health and happiness, and also allows you to get more done in less time.

Do Yoga: Another great example of mind-body cross training is yoga, which improves the strength, balance, and flexibility of the body while also improving your focus, attention, and mindfulness.[8] Researchers have begun to evaluate the brain's ability to learn and retain information while the body is engaged in physical activity,[9] and yoga is documented as benefiting well-being and refreshing the mind for higher performance.[10]

Go For Walks: Taking time for a stroll is definitely a good way to experience cognitive shifting, out of tense mind states into a more relaxed and creative state of mind, while also providing good physical activity. My personal experience is that doing light exercise such as walking on the treadmill or using an elliptical machine helps me focus when I'm trying to do research or be creative.

Stimulating circulation through walking increases blood flow to the brain, which may help boost retention. Having to focus on movement may also eliminate the brain drain of multiple distractions. When I read on the couch or in my office, my mind wanders. But when I read and walk on a treadmill (which also takes a bit of training and coordination), I am able to focus on what I'm reading.

Re-directing Your Automatic Pilot – For Good

The most important thing about endurance training is that it supports sustainable behavior change, so that you can continue your new brain-healthy lifestyle forever. It's so important to have a supportive story and a purpose that truly matters to you, to keep yourself motivated when times get tough. My dear friend Bill McAlpine gave me permission to share a story he uses to help him stay committed to his workout routine. It's one of my all-time favorites:

> "I travel a lot. It is part of the challenge of doing my job. The upside is that when I am home, I am home. Other than the occasional conference call, submitting invoices, and basic office work, my time is mine and I choose to spend as much of it as I can with my wife and two daughters.
>
> But I recognize that in order for me to be the best for my family, I need to first take care of myself. On the surface,

taking the time to work out, especially with my heavy work schedule, would appear selfish. In fact, those are the words of a small voice that wells up inside of me.

How do you silence that voice and make sure that you take care of the things you know are important, even if that means you need to spend a little more time away from the people who matter the most to you to do so? If you want to make change, my belief is that you have to change what you believe. You need to change your perception of your situation. If we believe that we are time bankrupt, and that taking care of our self by working out is a selfish act, we will behave accordingly. For me, I needed to change not only my perception of working out, but also the perception of my daughters.

Why do I work out – to look better or feel better? Do I do it just for the pure joy of it? (Hardly!) I found that none of these reasons were meaningful enough to sustain change. I had to change my perception. I needed to find a core value beyond what marketers, advertisements, or celebrities wanted me to believe mattered.

Why work out? It is an act of love. Never thought of it that way? Me neither. But as I thought about my 'why' for working out and eating right, I had to figure out what would help me sustain the change. I needed to find a way to make sure that no matter what the circumstances, I would take care of myself.

So I began my indoctrination. I reminded myself of the true reason I do these things – because I love my family.

I used this statement as my personal mantra. I shared these thoughts with my family. I began instilling in my daughters at a very young age that the reason why Mommy (my wife is very faithful in her workouts; for me it is an effort) and Daddy work out is because 'We love them, and we want to be around for them long-term.' My perception changed. My family's perception changed. Taking care of myself stopped being an act of selfishness, and became an act of love.

I knew the change stuck when on a warm central Texas July morning my youngest daughter asked me if I was going to work out today. I was lying on the couch and had no desire to work out. It was hot and I was tired – missing one day was no big deal. I turned to my daughter and simply replied, 'Naw, I don't think so.' I figured that was a good enough answer, and I could go back to more productive activities like watching TV.

My daughter's eyes began to water, and her lower lip started to quiver. She looked at me with her gorgeous brown eyes and said quietly, 'Don't you love me?' I felt like someone had just punched me in the gut and knocked all the wind out of me. I stood up and said, 'Grab my spandex. I'm riding.' The biggest smile came over her and she hugged me, saying, 'Thank you, Daddy.'

The small things really do matter. If you are like me, change may start with shifting your perception of why you do what you do. What do you believe? Simply stated, **anchor change in a core value in order to sustain it.**"

A Few More Endurance Builders

In addition to establishing a strong sense of purpose and making sure your story supports it, there are a few more things to keep in mind when it comes to making your plan sustainable long-term: setting goals that are 'SMART,' celebrating small wins, and adding accountability.

1) Set SMART Goals

It's important to regularly set and evaluate both short-term goals and long-term goals. And remember that in 'SMART' format, goals should be:

- Specific

- Measurable

- Actionable

- Realistic

- Timed

These five requirements will allow you to be clear regarding what you are doing, to keep track of your progress, and to stay confident that the goal is attainable within a certain period of time.

Once you start your training program, please pay close attention, each day and each week, to how you're progressing – so that you can make adjustments as needed.

Common mistakes include:

- Taking on too many goals at one time

- Taking on goals that are too lofty

- Not being specific enough about goals or behaviors

- Not being flexible when circumstances change

In your log, you are always free to change any of your goals and exercises that you find not appropriate based on the above considerations. Your life is constantly changing, and in order for you to keep up with your daily and weekly training program, your goals will also need to be adaptable. This flexibility will allow you to adjust your plan rather than abandon it.

2) Celebrate Small Wins

People often get frustrated when they set out on a new training program and follow all of the recommendations, but don't seem to see much progress right away. Many times this lack of perceived momentum is linked to a goal that's too difficult to reach in a realistic period of time. (Weight loss is a great example of a training goal that people can quickly give up on when the scale doesn't move fast enough.)

Rather than focus on attaining the final outcome, it may be helpful to break a lofty goal into smaller goals, so that you can see the progress you're making, and stop to celebrate your success along the way.

It's all too easy to get stuck pushing toward future goals, and to move right from one goal to the next, forgetting that establishing the first set of habits was a big deal. Having small wins along the way helps you see progress and stay motivated.

This brings up an important consideration: Are you running your life so that you're always pushing to get to your next goal (future-oriented living), or are you running your life to enjoy the moment-to-moment process of life itself? This issue might be a giant mindset shift for you, if you're overly goal-oriented.

One of the wonderful impacts of meditating regularly is that you focus more on the present moment process and enjoyment of each new breath, and let go of trying to constantly 'run after the carrot.'

The exercises in this book have been designed to be a pleasure to do. So don't try to push ahead into the future – instead, try to enjoy each moment of doing them.

See if you can set a goal to learn how to enjoy each moment more, and you'll find that your entire life expands, relaxes, becomes filled with more meaning and hope, and boosts your mental performance and overall success in life.

3) Build Accountability

A key to consistency with these exercises is holding yourself accountable. You are now assuming full responsibility for your cognitive health and clarity. There are no more teachers standing over you, watching to see if you perform – it's all up to you. By focusing on and working with your training log regularly, you are making yourself accountable to yourself. This is so important!

However, it's also easy to play mind games with yourself and come up with all sorts of excuses as to why you simply cannot stick with your regimen right now. Although there is usually an element of truth to every story, we need to see if that story is really working for us or against us.

What's to be done about this?

- First of all, you can decide to get really honest with yourself, and start to identify and re-write the stories you might be using to get you off the hook. Remember, it takes practice not only to hear what you're telling yourself, but also to come up with a better script that will better support your efforts.

- Also, you can tell someone else about your goals. It helps to make your exercise intent known to others, it makes your plans more real, and makes your goals public record. You also tap into social support, which can be significant in achieving your aims.

- You might want to determine specifically how you will check in (e-mail, phone, in person) and when you'll check in (every day, every Friday, at staff meetings) with your accountability partner, coach, or group.

- You can also build in rewards if you think they will be helpful for you (a special lunch or massage once a week, or a vacation day).

A great sense of accomplishment can be achieved that boosts your self esteem and strengthens your story, as you become more responsible for setting goals and carrying through with them.

To see a video of author Heidi Hanna talking about accountability for mental endurance, scan the QR code below

Top Techniques for Training Mental Endurance

Here are more suggestions of what you can do every day to make your life feel fuller and your brain more clear and powerful, now and into the future:

1) Have More Fun

Life really should be more fun for all of us! And one of the best ways to improve compliance with any program is to enjoy what you're doing. Many of the experts I consulted for this book suggested finding ways to make training strategies fun, so that you are more likely to want to keep doing them, as opposed to feeling like you're punishing yourself. Again, it's all about mind over matter, and developing attitudes that optimize your goals.

Physical exercise is a great example. When you have to drag yourself out of bed to get to the gym, it often feels like torture, and your brain can easily talk you out of going with a million reasons why it's not such a good idea after all: "I need more sleep," "I'll get to it later," "I'll start again tomorrow," and so on.

Instead of thinking about all the negatives in this situation, you can begin to remember all the times when you were feeling good while exercising. You do have the power to focus on the positive, and this is a great example – try it!

Playing sports that you enjoy is another great way to do cross training for the brain and body. Whenever possible, choose sports that challenge your cardiovascular system while also challenging your mind. These activities will increase the strength of your brain cells, while also forming more complex connections between them. Not only does that keep you mentally stimulated, it also increases social connection.

2) Laugh Out Loud

Remember, laughter is beneficial in multiple ways:

Physically, laughter stimulates most of the same endorphins (brain chemicals) as exercise and can increase blood flow and energy production.

Mentally, laughter helps us to get a nice break from stress and stimulates the relaxation response inside our body and mind.

During your mental recharge breaks, why not find something funny to think about. Watch a silly movie clip or a video of friends or family playing. Listen to a few minutes of a comedy show or audio book. Tell a joke, or ask someone to tell you one. Or check out a website with funny comics or videos such as http://www.funnyordie.com, http://www.break.com, or http://www.theonion.com.

3) Walking Meditation

You don't need to be sitting still to take a mental time-out. Going for a stroll is a great way to boost physical activity, relax your mind, and engage in social connection with someone you enjoy spending time with.

Or, if you prefer to walk alone you can use this time to meditate on one of your focus phrases, or simply practice being in the moment with enhanced mindfulness. Listening to soft music or serene background noise like waves crashing or a waterfall can help quiet your mind during your walking meditation.

4) Practice Yoga

As we discussed earlier, yoga is a great cross-training strategy, which improves the strength, balance, and flexibility of the body and the mind.[11] Many quality studies have shown that practicing yoga benefits the whole person, and it has been proven to decrease anxiety and stress levels,[12] improve aerobic capacity,[13] and enhance better quality of sleep. When used in combination with breathing exercises, it may be beneficial in treating chemical dependency and alcoholism.[14] Yoga also appears to be a good way to cope with chronic pain and minimize the negative effects of breast cancer and diabetes.[15]

Just like breathing exercises, practicing yoga can elicit a return to homeostasis (balance) by initiating the relaxation response.

Yoga typically moves through a variety of 'asanas,' or poses that awaken a greater sense of body awareness. There are many different types of Yoga, utilizing different methods of moving in and out of strategic poses such as Hatha, Ashtanga, power yoga, Bikram, and Iyengar. I would suggest trying a few different styles with a few different instructors to determine the best fit for you. Most gyms offer at least a couple different types of yoga, and you can also use videos online or on a DVD.

There are even some programs that offer a live online version of yoga such as emindful.com, myyogaonline, and yogajournal.com.

5) Do Some Good

According to Dr. Seligman and his colleagues at the University of Pennsylvania, doing something kind for someone else produces the single most reliable momentary increase in well-being.[16] Of all the positive psychology strategies tested by his team, going into your community and doing something helpful for another person produced the largest increase in happiness – and the positive effects lasted for a month.

A great way to boost positivity while adding a stronger sense of purpose to your training program is to pause regularly, reflect on the people in your life, and decide to be helpful to one of them during the next week.

Once you start looking, you'll begin finding loads of ways in which you can be of significant help to people around you. One of the most direct ways to be helpful is to get involved with a charity that you believe in. There are so many good causes that would love your support. By signing up for an event that also benefits someone else, you increase your positivity, sense of purpose, and social connections, all while training your brain and your body.

SHARP Sprints

The following are quick activities that support mental endurance:

Define Your Daily Purpose

Answer the following questions: "My purpose in life is..." and then "My purpose for today is..."

Do an Intentional Act of Kindness

Create a ritual to do one nice thing for someone every day. Plan it out and track it, in order to establish a new habit.

Add Additional Accountability

Don't keep your training plan a secret – bring it up regularly to people outside your official accountability group. Each time you share with someone, you boost your motivation, commitment, and compliance.

Treat Yourself

Non-caloric treats are a fun way to make sure your motivation stays fired up without packing on the pounds or causing a sugar induced energy roller coaster. Examples might be a new pair of jeans, a massage, new music, or even just scheduling an extra break each day for a week to go for a relaxing walk.

Quick Cross-training Boost

Activities like journaling, meditation, visualization, biofeedback, skills-based physical activity, socializing around hobbies, and playing sports provide benefit in multiple dimensions – body, mind, and spirit. Remember every little effort you invest in yourself will help boost the energy you have to give to the people around you, and it all adds up over time.

Training Take Away

To build resilience, we must have a consistent program that we can use on a regular basis and that we will be able to maintain over time. **Remember, we're doing more than just adding years to our life – we're adding life to our years**! Training your brain to be stronger and more resilient is **endurance training**, which allows you to bring your best mental energy to the present moment and for many years to come.

CHAPTER 12
Create Your *SHARP* Training Plan

As we approach the finish line of this book, it's your turn to take action, make decisions, and to determine what your next steps will be.

In order to develop a *SHARP* brain, you will need to create a strategic plan that will maximize your return on investment. To do that, you will want to utilize training principles that will work effectively, and then follow the *SHARP* Strategies to keep your training consistent and sustainable.

To see a video of author Heidi Hanna talking about the SHARP Strategies, scan the QR code below

To stay sharp, it's important to have a plan that provides structure for the journey ahead. So, when designing your plan, keep the following concepts in mind:

S – Schedule it: If it's important to us, we plan it. Most of us manage our schedules for work, but fail to put in planning time for the rest of our life. Be sure to keep your strategies simple so that it is realistic for you to incorporate them into your busy schedule. Setting an alarm is a helpful reminder that can also snap you out of work mode for a moment to help you make your self-care practice a priority.

H – Helpful tools: There are a lot of tools available to facilitate your training by providing guidance, support, and accountability. You may need to spend some time trying different things until you find something that works just right for you. Several options are listed in the resources section of this book.

A – Accountability: As we just reviewed, one of the best ways to increase compliance with any training program is to build in accountability with yourself, and ideally with other people you care about. Sharing your log will boost your level of commitment because it's harder to slack off when someone else is monitoring your progress.

R – Routine: As much as possible, use strategies that you can incorporate into your current routine. For example, if you want to remember to take your vitamins, set them out by your coffee pot, since your auto-brain is already driving you in that direction in the morning. Store healthier food options where they're easy to find, and make your splurge foods harder to get to. Keep an extra set of walking shoes at your office where you can see them.

P – Practice: Any new behavior is going to take an investment of time and energy in order to make it a habit, so design your training plan using the previous suggestions – and then practice, practice, practice. Schedule time-specific exercise time into your day and make it a priority.

There you have it ... the *S.H.A.R.P.* program. Return to these five key points regularly to make sure you're on target with your training strategy.

I am now going to list in one short presentation all of this book's general suggestions about building a healthy foundation, along with the specific brain fitness exercises we've discussed, so that you can begin to develop your training log. This log will be your daily reminder to make healthy choices, challenge your brain, and get adequate recovery. To do this successfully, you'll want to work either with a training log of your choice, or utilize your computer's scheduling program.

Create Your Training Log

1) First of all, before 'doing' anything, quiet your mind by taking a few calming breaths ... and ask yourself what your primary purpose is in beginning a brain fitness program.

2) Now, while you stay in tune with your breathing and your deeper purpose, read through all the suggestions and exercises reprinted here ... and **write down** the ones that most interest you. Go back and re-read any of the exercise discussions in the book that you're not sure of.

3) Indicate in writing, for each exercise, how many times a week you might do this exercise, and how many minutes you would like to devote to it.

4) Decide how many total minutes each day you are willing to commit to doing your full brain fitness program.

5) Now **rank order the exercises** that interest you on your list, starting with the most important as #1.

6) Evaluating total time, choose the top rated exercises that will fit into your time schedule.

7) Pause, review this whole process to make sure you have a balanced program, and make any changes or substitutions you want to.

8) **Create a formal list** of the exercises you're going to begin training with, and **enter these into your log** by specific date and time.

9) Sit quietly and meditate on your list and your decision to discipline yourself to accomplish your stated goals. Make sure that you feel good about your strategy. If not, review again.

10) Once your program design is complete, take time to determine how you will hold yourself accountable. If at all possible, **share your goals and strategy** with an accountability partner or group right away.

To implement your *SHARP* brain training strategy, check your log tomorrow morning to see what's on your schedule. Establish a habit to look at your training log at the same time and place each day. And ... here you go!

Brain Health Fundamentals

#1: Fuel Better

1. Eat something every 3–4 hours
2. Consume low-glycemic snacks throughout the day (determine specific times for snack breaks on your log)
3. Choose meals that are 50% fruits and vegetables, 25% lean protein, and 25% complex carbohydrates
4. Eat portion sizes that leave you feeling satisfied, and not full
5. Eat high nutrient value foods the majority of the time (aim for 90/10)

#2: Move More

1. Get up and move your body at least every 90 minutes
2. Accumulate 60 minutes of general activity during the day
3. Get 30 minutes of moderate to high intensity cardiovascular exercise a minimum of 3x a week
4. Do full body strength training exercises at least 2x a week
5. Stretch daily

#3: Balance Stress

1. See that stress is necessary, and keep challenging yourself
2. Appreciate the need for recovery, and schedule *SHARP* Recharge Breaks to relax, rebalance, and recharge (3x/day)
3. Take breaks at least every 90 minutes for optimal oscillation
4. Practice relaxation strategies daily
5. Keep relaxation/recovery appointments in your log a priority

#4: *Get A Good Night's Sleep*

1. Go to bed early

2. Practice sleep inducing meditation

3. Avoid caffeine late in the day

4. Limit or abstain from drinking alcohol before bed

5. Wind down by limiting computer use and other stimulating activities before bed.

#5: *Feel More Connected*

1. Schedule lunch with a colleague or friend once a week

2. Set up a weekly date night with your partner or spouse

3. Schedule a date night with one of your children once a week

4. Plan to call home at a certain time each day to connect with family

5. Take a class, join a club or sports team, or participate in a networking event once a week

Real World Brain Training Exercises

Exercise #1: Basic 'Here & Now' Breath Meditation

This exercise utilizes breath awareness to improve your connection between the mind and the body.

Exercise #2: Shift Into 'Zero-Task' Mode

Quiet down and focus your mind with breath awareness plus basic focusing meditation.

Exercise #3: The Expanded Brain Recharge Process

This 3-minute brain recharge utilizes meditation to help recover, rebalance, and recharge your mental energy. Recommended tools include:

- Using basic breath awareness

- Repeating a focus phrase

- Focusing the mind on a picture or object

- Watching or listening to a video or audio track

- Counting breaths and holding attention on breathing

Exercise #4: Distraction Resistance

Remember, turn it off or tune it out!

Exercise #5: Mental Rehearsal

Think of something you'd like to improve upon, and use mental rehearsal to practice for success.

Exercise #6: Use a Training Log

Write down specific steps for your plan and track progress.

Exercise #7: Chunk Your Day

To avoid multitasking, chunk your day into time blocks where you can focus your attention fully for shorter segments of time.

Exercise #8: 5-minute Laser Focus

Set a timer for 5 minutes, go to work with total focus, and get as much of that task done as you can without allowing any disruptions.

Exercise #9: Challenge Yourself

Think of something you usually do on automatic pilot and do it differently (use your non-dominant hand to eat, wash your hair, or brush your teeth; drive a new route to work, etc).

Exercise #10: Move It, Move It

Set your timer for 2-3 minutes and do a quick exercise or two in order to get your heart pumping, boost brain chemicals, and circulate oxygen and glucose to the brain.

Exercise #11: Count Down, Count Up

Choose a counting exercise, such as starting at 100 and counting down by 5 at a time. When you get good at this, try more difficult numbers like 7.

Exercise #12: Red Dot Experience

Place a few red dot stickers around your workplace or home, and each time you see one commit to increasing your mindfulness by bringing your attention to the here and now, and tuning into your breathing.

Exercise #13: Get Your Story Right

Commit to spending a few minutes identifying your negative assumptions, and then choose to begin reinforcing the opposite statement or belief (such as changing "taking care of myself is selfish," to "taking care of myself is critical for me to take care of others").

Exercise #14: Practice Gratitude

Each morning, write down three things you're grateful for. For more of a positivity boost, also share what you're grateful for each evening with someone you care about.

Exercise #15: Makeover Your Mindset

Think of a negative assumption and practice saying it in a more positive way (such as turning "things are falling apart right now" into "this is a challenge, and I'll be stronger because of it").

Exercise #16: Quiet Your Mind

Spend 3–5 minutes turning your focus of attention to the experience of your breathing, letting go of any thoughts that are trying to grab your attention, and enjoy the silence.

Exercise #17: Motivate With Mantras

Come up with a personal mantra, write it down, post it where you can see it often, and reflect on it regularly throughout the day.

Exercise #18: Thank You or Just Because Note

Jot a quick note to a relative, friend or colleague, or someone you just met to show appreciation or let them know you're thinking of them.

Exercise #19: Visualization

Think through something you'd like to improve on in as much detail as you can. Use all the senses to provide a true-to-life mental experience, including how you want to feel as an outcome of the particular task or experience.

Exercise #20: Short Guided Imagery

Use an audio track to guide you through a relaxing, focusing, or energizing process (samples available at www.synergyprograms. com/braingym).

Exercise #21: Look Back and Forth

Write down a few things that happened recently that you are thankful for and a few things you are looking forward to in the near future.

Exercise #22: Rewrite a Short Story

When in a challenging situation, quickly write down negative bullet points and see if you can reframe them in a more positive way.

Exercise #23: Have More Fun

Find ways to incorporate more fun and play into your routine, such as getting together with friends, going to a comedy club or a funny movie, or joining a sports team or club.

Exercise #24: Laugh Out Loud

Watch a silly movie clip or a video of friends or family playing, listen to a few minutes of a comedy show or audio book, tell a joke, or ask someone to tell you one. Check out a website with funny comics or videos.

Exercise #25: Walking Meditation

Go for a stroll to boost physical activity, relax your mind, and possibly engage in social connection with someone you enjoy spending time with.

Exercise #26: Practice Yoga

Try a yoga class at a gym, using a video, or in an online classroom.

Exercise #27: Do Some Good

Choose someone in your life and come up with a way to do something helpful for him or her. Or sign up for a charity fundraiser or fitness event.

Exercise #28: Write Down Your Purpose for Today

Finish the following statements and then write down the answers where you can see them regularly throughout the day: "My purpose in life is…" and then "My purpose for today is…."

Exercise #29: Add Additional Accountability

Talk to people around you regularly about what you're working on to make your goal feel more real, and to boost your accountability.

Exercise #30: Treat Yourself

Come up with a reward for completing your training program each day, week, or month.

Exercise #31: Cross-Train

Pick a strategy that incorporates more than one aspect of fitness such as journaling, positive meditation, yoga – or physical exercises that incorporate coordination and balance.

Now that you have read through and written down the exercises that interest you, here's a reminder of what to do next:

1) Indicate, for each exercise on your list, how many times a week you might do this exercise, and how many minutes you'd devote to it.

2) Decide how many total minutes each day you are willing to commit to doing your full brain fitness program.

3) Now rank order the exercises that interest you on your list, starting with the most important as #1.

4) Evaluating total time, choose the top rated exercises that will fit into your time schedule.

5) Pause, review this whole process to make sure you have a balanced program, and make any changes or substitutions you want to.

6) Create a formal list of the exercises you're going to start your brain fitness program with, and enter these into your log by specific date and time.

7) Sit quietly and meditate on your list, and your decision to discipline yourself to accomplish your stated goals. Make sure that you feel good about your strategy. If not, review again.

8) Once your program design is complete, determine how you will hold yourself accountable. If at all possible, share your goals and strategy with an accountability partner or group.

Once you fulfill this list, you are ready to implement your *SHARP* training program into your real life. Tomorrow morning, make sure to pause and read your log, to see what's first on your schedule. Establish a habit each morning to review your log, at the same time and place, and you're off and running.

Keep in mind that every journey begins with taking that first step, and you've already done that by investigating ways to keep yourself sharp. You've started training already! You've started training already! Now, be focused, flexible, and consistent as you begin working on this routine to keep your brain *SHARP*, so that you enjoy a healthy, happy, and successful life for a very long time to come.

AFTERWARD: My Story

Most authors start a book like this one with a personal story or an explanation of what makes them an expert on the topic. But I've decided to save that part for last because this book is not about me. It's about you. However, I've learned over the last decade of coaching, speaking, and traveling that we all learn from each other, and having authentic conversations is an important part of making a deep connection. So, I would like to share a bit about my story and goals, and why this book is an important part of my personal life mission.

As I have mentioned, mental strength training has enabled me to face two of my biggest fears on a regular basis: flying and public speaking. In fact, when I first took on the job as a performance coach and trainer, I told my interviewer that I had absolutely no interest in ever traveling for work, nor in getting up on a stage. Up to that point, the only way I could persuade myself to get on an airplane was when I had to travel to visit my family, or to keep my softball scholarship in college – and I continued to be a 'white knuckle' traveler the whole time.

I had to learn how to change my mindset to think in entirely new ways in order to continue my professional journey, which included frequent airplane flights and regular lectures on stage. I still consistently practice these strategies so I can continue on this path, because I feel a strong connection to the purpose of what I am doing.

Goal #1: Develop a stronger brain to take me where I want to go.

Resilience became a critical factor in keeping my professional journey moving forward when I suddenly found myself in the hospital twice in one week for unknown reasons. The level of anxiety I was experiencing with all the traveling and speaking was so intense that when I became injured and couldn't exercise, the toxic stress hormones became overwhelming, and my system just quit. I became physically exhausted and experienced severe anxiety that lasted for weeks. At that point I thought I'd have to quit my job because there seemed to be no other solution.

Fortunately, friends and family rallied around me and reminded me that I was stronger than I thought, and that I had been given an amazing career opportunity that I couldn't give up without a good fight.

Now, eight years, hundreds of presentations, and over a dozen international trips later, I still get sweaty palms sometimes. I still have an energy crash from time to time, and find myself getting out of balance. But maintaining self-care rituals, balancing stress and recovery, and keeping up with consistent nutrition and exercise practices have become part of my job description, and the job description of the other members of my team (a monthly massage, or other spa service, is mandatory and reimbursed).

Goal #2: Figure out how to be more resilient to stress.

I had another shock to my system when I first experienced losing a loved one to Alzheimer's disease. I had always been interested in brain health and performance, but it wasn't until I spent time with my grandmother as she was dying that I fully realized the magnitude of what brain disease can rob from us. As it turns out, I have several grandparents who have suffered from this disease.

222

This personal connection had made promoting awareness of this disease a critical element of my personal and professional work.

Brain disease not only attacks one's body, it attacks one's soul. As the mind deteriorates, one's personality changes drastically, and someone who was once sweet, loving, and kind can become angry, irritable, and mean. (Thankfully, I did not experience this with any of my family members.) Impulse control goes away, and bizarre behaviors start to manifest as the brain malfunctions.

For someone who invests a great amount in self-improvement and education, the thought of this perhaps happening to me really shook me up. I contacted my local Alzheimer's Association chapter and volunteered to help promote awareness and prevention efforts, which is part of my personal mission in writing this book.

While there is still no treatment for Alzheimer's disease and other forms of dementia, studies consistently show that we may be able to prevent or at least delay the development of these diseases through the brain health and fitness strategies discussed in this book. I call this my "sneak attack" to making people healthier – learn to optimize performance, and become healthier as a side effect.

Goal #3: Learn how to age gracefully while maintaining my mental focus, clarity, and optimism, and do everything I can to keep the people I love as healthy as possible.

So, for your own sake, the people you love, and those who might end up as your caregivers in the future, I encourage you to spend daily time keeping your own brain in top shape! Wishing you all the health, happiness, and success in life you can possibly stand.

HH

RESOURCES: Helpful Websites and Apps

The *SHARP* Brain Gym – www.synergyprograms.com/braingym

The Daily Plate – Food and Exercise Tracking Program:
www.livestrong.com/thedailyplate

Sleep Stream – Guided Meditations and relaxation tracks:
http://sleepstream.explosiveapps.com/

MyBrainSolutions – Brain Exercises, Relaxation Room and
My Calm Beat breathing and biofeedback program:
www.mybrainsolutions.com/sharp

HeartMath – Biofeedback devices and research:
www.heartmathstore.com

For More Information

Alzheimer's Association: www.alz.org

American Dietetic Association: www.eatright.org

American Psychological Association: www.apa.org

Recommended Reading

Brain Plasticity and Brain Training
Brain Rules – John Medina
Mindsight – Daniel Siegel
The Talent Code – Daniel Coyle
Willpower – Roy Baumeister
Think Smart – Richard Restak
Buddha's Brain – Rick Hanson
Mindset – Carol Dweck
Positivity – Barbara Fredrickson
Rapt – Winifred Gallagher

Nutrition
The *SHARP* Diet – Heidi Hanna and Tara Gidus
Change Your Brain, Change Your Body – Daniel Amen
In Defense of Food – Michael Pollan
Mindless Eating – Brian Wansink
The Beck Diet Solution – Judith Beck
The End of Overeating – David Kessler

Physical Activity and Exercise
SPARK – John Ratey

Stress
Why Zebras Don't Get Ulcers – Robert Sapolsky
The How of Happiness – Sonja Lyubomirsky
Getting Things Done – David Allen
The Effective Executive – Peter Drucker

Purpose
The Power of Full Engagement – Jim Loehr & Tony Schwartz
The Power of Purpose – Richard Leider
Believe Me – Michael Margolis
The Power of Story – Jim Loehr

Sleep
Sleep For Success – James Maas

Social Connection
Loneliness – John Cacioppo & William Patrick

Healthy Aging
The Blue Zones – Dan Buettner
Counterclockwise – Ellen Langer
Flourish – Martin Seligman
Younger Next Year – Chris Crowley & Henry Lodge

REFERENCES

Chapter 1

1) Smith, G. E., Housen, P., Yaffe, K., Ruff, R., Kennison, R. F., Mahncke, H. W., & Zelinski, E. M. (2009), A Cognitive Training Program Based on Principles of Brain Plasticity: Results from the Improvement in Memory with Plasticity-based Adaptive Cognitive Training (IMPACT) Study. *Journal of the American Geriatrics Society, 57,* 594–603.

2) Danner, Snowdon, & Friesen, (2001). Positive Emotions in Early Life and Longevity: Findings from the Nun Study. *Journal of Personality and Social Psychology, 80* (5), 804-813.

3) Brown, K., (2003). The benefits of being present: Mindfulness and its role in psychological well-being. *Journal of Personality and Social Psychology, 84,* 822-848.

4) Clapp, W., Rubens, Sabharwal, J., & Gazzaley, A. (published ahead of print April 11, 2011) Deficit in switching between functional brain networks underlies the impact of multitasking on working memory in older adults, *Proceedings of the National Academy of Sciences,* 108 (17) 7212-7217

5) Just, M., Keller, T., & Cynkar, J. (April, 2008). A decrease in brain activation associated with driving when listening to someone speak. *Brain Research, 205,* (18), 70-80. Retrieved from: http://www.sciencedirect.com/science/article/pii/S0006899308002989

6) Ophir, E., Nass, C., & Wagner, A. D. (August, 2009). Cognitive control in media multitaskers. *Proceedings of the National Academy of Sciences, 106* (37): 15583–7.

7) Hanson, R., (2009). *Buddha's Brain: The Practical Neuroscience of Happiness, Love, and Wisdom.* Oakland, CA: New Harbinger Publications.

8) Adams, J., (2009). Cost Savings from Health Promotion and Stress Management Interventions. *OD Practitioner, 41 (4),* 31-37.

9) Families and Work Institute, (2008). The State of Health in the American Workforce: Does having an effective workplace matter? Retrieved from www.familiesandwork.org.

10) Alzheimer's Association, (2011). 2011 Alzheimer's Disease Facts and Figures, *Alzheimer's and Dementia, 7* (2), 12.

11) Alzheimer's Association, (2011). 2011 Alzheimer's Disease Facts and Figures, *Alzheimer's and Dementia, 7* (2), 21.

12) Snowdon, D., (1997). Aging and Alzheimer's Disease: Lessons From the Nun Study. *The Gerontologist, 37 (2)*, 150-156.

13) Buettner, D., (2008). *The Blue Zones: Lessons for Living Longer From the People Who've Lived the Longest.* Washington, DC: National Geographic Books.

Chapter 2

1) Ratey, J., with Hagerman, E., (2008). *Spark: The Revolutionary Science of Exercise and the Brain.* New York, NY: Little, Brown and Company.

2) Loehr, J., & Schwartz, T., (2003). *The Power of Full Engagement: Managing Energy, Not Time, is the Key to High Performance and Personal Renewal.* New York, NY: Free Press.

Chapter 4

1) Fernandez, A., & Goldberg, E., (2009). *The Guide to Brain Fitness: 18 interviews with scientists, practical advice, and product reviews, to keep your brain sharp.* Retrieved from http://www.sharpbrains.com/book/

2) Buettner, D., (2008). *The Blue Zones: Lessons for Living Longer From the People Who've Lived the Longest.* Washington, DC: National Geographic Books.

3) Williams, J., Plassman, B., Burke, J., Holsinger, T., & Benjamin S., (April 2010). Preventing Alzheimer's Disease and Cognitive Decline. Evidence Report/ Technology Assessment No. 193. Rockville, MD: Agency for Healthcare Research and Quality.

4) Scarmeas, N., et al. (August 2009). Physical Activity, Diet, and risk of Alzheimer disease. *JAMA, 302*(6), 627-37.

5) Restak, R., (2009). *Think Smart: A Neuroscientist's Prescription for Improving Your Brain's Performance.* New York, NY: Riverhead Books.

6) Lopez, O., Becker, J., Kuller, L., Ho, A., Parikshak, N., Hua, X., Leow, A., & Toga, A., (2009). Obesity Bad for the Brain: Mapping Study Suggests Brain Shrinkage in Obese Elderly Could Increase Alzheimer's Risk.

7) Xu, W., Atti, A., Gatz, , M., Pedersen, N., Johnson, B., & Fratiglioni, L., (2011). Midlife overweight and obesity increase late-life dementia risk: A population-based twin study. *Neurology, 76 (18)*, 1568-1574.

Chapter 5

1) Medina, J., (2009). *Brain Rules.* Seattle, WA: Pear Press.

2) Patel, A.V., Bernstein, L., Deka, A., Feigelson, H.S., Campbell, P.T., Gapstur, S.M., Colditz, G.A., & Thun, M.J., (2010). Leisure Time Spent Sitting in Relation to Total Mortality in a Prospective Cohort of US Adults. *American Journal of Epidemiology, 172* (4), 419-429.

3) Ferris, L. T., Williams, J.S., & Shen, C.L., (2007). The effect of acute exercise on serum brain-derived neurotrophic factor levels and cognitive function. Med. Sci. Sports Exerc., Vol. 39, No. 4, pp. 728–734

4) Colcombe, S., Erickson, K., Scalf, P., Kim, J., & Prakash, R., (2006). Exercise: An Active Route to Healthy Aging Aerobic Exercise Training Increases Brain Volume in Aging Humans. *Journal of Gerontology: Medical Sciences, 61 A* (11), 1166-1170.

5) Yaffe, K., Barnes, D., Nevitt, M., Lui, L., & Covinsky, K., (2001). A Prospective Study of Physical Activity and Cognitive Decline in Elderly Women: Women Who Walk. *Arch Intern Med, 161,* 1703-1708.

6) Colcombe, S., Kramer, A., Erickson, K., Scalf, P., McAuley, E., Cohen, N., Webb, A., Jerome, G., Marquez, D., & Elavsky, S., (2004). Cardiovascular fitness, cortical plasticity, and aging. *PNAS, 101(9),* 3316-3321.

7) Ratey, J., with Hagerman, E., (2008). *Spark: The Revolutionary Science of Exercise and the Brain.* New York, NY: Little, Brown and Company.

8) Wellness Councils of America, (1995). Corporate Leaders Laud Benefits of Wellness. *Worksite Wellness Works,* May.

9) Steyn, N., (2004). Diet, nutrition and the prevention of type 2 diabetes. *Public Health Nutrition, 7(1A),* 147–165.

10) Haskell, W., et al, (2007). Physical Activity and Public Health: Updated Recommendation for Adults from the American College of Sports Medicine and the American Heart Association. *Med Sci Sports Exerc, 39,* (8), 1423–1434.

11) Tanasescu, M., (2002). Exercise type and intensity in relation to coronary heart disease in men. *JAMA; 288(16),* 1994–2000.

Chapter 6

1) Ratey, J., with Hagerman, E., (2008). *Spark: The Revolutionary Science of Exercise and the Brain.* New York, NY: Little, Brown and Company.

2) Sapolsky, R., (2004). *Why Zebras Don't Get Ulcers (3ʳᵈ Edition).* New York, NY: Holt Paperbacks.

3) *Golf Digest,* (Oct 2010). How to Train Your Brain: Good thinking might beat out a good stroke.

Chapter 7

1) The Better Sleep Council, (2007). Position Statement: Poor Sleep Affecting Accuracy And Attitude On The Job *New National Better Sleep Month Survey Highlights Link between Sleep and Work Performance.* Retrieved from http://www.bettersleep.org/Pressroom/press-release.aspx?id=4

2) Ferrie, J., et al, (2011). Change in sleep duration and cognitive function: findings from the Whitehall II study. *Sleep, 34 (5)*, 565-573.

3) Maas, J.B., Robbins, R.S., & Dement, W.C., (2010) *Sleep for Success: Everything You Must Know About Sleep but Are too Tired to Ask.* Bloomington, IN: AuthorHouse.

4) Basner, M., & Dinges, D., (2011). Maximizing sensitivity of the psychomotor vigilance test (PVT) to sleep loss. *Sleep, 34(5)*, 581-591.

5) Van Dongen, H., Rogers, N.L., & Dinges, D.F., (2003). Sleep debt: Theoretical and empirical issues. *Sleep and Biological Rhythms, 1* (1), 5-13.

6) National Center for Health Statistics, (2008). Sleep Duration as a Correlate of Smoking, Alcohol Use, Leisure-Time Physical Inactivity, and Obesity Among Adults: United States, 2004-2006. Retrieved from http://www.cdc.gov/nchs/data/hestat/sleep04-06/sleep04-06.htm

Chapter 8

1) Holt-Lunstad J., Smith T., & Layton J., (2010). Social Relationships and Mortality Risk: A Meta-analytic Review. *PloS Med, 7(7)*, 1-20.

2) Vaillant, G., (2009). Yes, I stand by my words, Happiness equals love- full stop. Retrieved on January 26, 2011 from: www.positivepsychologynews.com

3) Cacioppo, J. & Patrick, W., (2008). *Loneliness: Human Nature and the Need for Social Connection.* New York, NY: W.W. Norton & Company.

4) Reis, H., & Gable, S., (2003). Toward a Positive Psychology of Relationships. In Keyes, C., and Haidt, J., (2003). *Flourishing: Positive Psychology and the Life Well-Lived.* Washington, DC: American Psychological Association.

5) Ybarra, O., Bernstein, E., Winkielman, P., Keller, M., Manis, M., Chan, E., & Rodriguez, J., (2008). Mental Exercising Through Simple Socializing: Social Interaction Promotes General Cognitive Functioning. *PSPB, 34 (2)*, 248-259.

6) Hawkley, L. Masi, M., Berry, D., & Cacioppo, T., (2006). Loneliness is a unique predictor of age-related differences in systolic blood pressure. *Psychology and Aging 21(1)*, 152 – 164.

7) Berkman, L., Leo-Summers, L., & Horwitz, R., (1992). Emotional Support and Survival after Myocardial Infarction: A Prospective, Population-based Study of the Elderly. *Ann Intern Med, 117, (12)*, 1003-1009.

8) Bloom, J., (2001). Sources of support and the physical and mental well-being of young women with breast cancer. *Social Science & Medicine, 53 (11)*, 1513-1524.

9) Rath, T., & Harter, J., (2010). *Wellbeing: The Five Essential Elements.* Washington, DC: Gallup Press.

Chapter 9

1) Dean, D., & Webb, C., (Jan 2011). Recovering from information overload: Always-on, multitasking work environments are killing productivity, dampening creativity, and making us unhappy. Retrieved from http://www.mckinseyquarterly.com/Recovering_from_information_overload_2735

2) Asplund, C., Dux, P., Ivanoff, J., & Marois, R., (2006). Isolation of a central bottleneck of information processing with time-resolved fMRI. *Neuron, 52, (6),* 1109–1120.

3) Reuters Business Information. (1996). *Dying for information? An investigation into the effects of information overload in the UK and worldwide.* London: Reuters Business Information.

4) Shellenbarger, S., (Feb 2003). Wall Street Journal: Multitasking Makes You Stupid: Studies Show Pitfalls of Doing Too Much at Once. Retrieved from https://www.wallstreetjournal.com

5) Gallagher, W., (2009). *Rapt: Attention and the Focused Life.* New York, NY: Penguin Press.

6) Baumeister, R.F., Gailliot, M., DeWall, C.N., & Oaten, M., (2006). Self-Regulation and Personality: How Interventions Increase Regulatory Success, and How Depletion Moderates the Effects of Traits on Behavior. *Journal of Personality, 74* (6).

7) González, V., & Mark, G., (2004). Constant, Constant, Multi-tasking Craziness": Managing Multiple Working Spheres. *CHI04, 6 (1).*

8) Gallup Management Journal, (2006). Too Many Interruptions at Work? Retrieved from http://gmj.gallup.com/content/23146/too-many-interruptions-work.aspx

9) Allen, D., (2002). *Getting Things Done: The Art of Stress-Free Productivity.* New York, NY: Penguin.

10) Drucker, P., (1967). *The Effective Executive.* New York, NY: HarperCollins Publisher.

11) Pascual-Leone A., (2001). The brain that plays music and is changed by it. Ann NY *Acad Sci, 930,* 315-329.

12) Cilley, M., (2002). *Sink Reflections.* New York, NY: Bantam Books.

Chapter 10

1) Levy, B., et al, (2002). Longevity increased by positive self-perceptions of aging. *Journal of Personality and Social Psychology, 83(2),* 261-270.

2) Langer, E., (2009). *Counterclockwise: Mindful Health and the Power of Possibility.* New York, NY: Ballantine Books.

3) Loehr, J., (2007). *The Power of Story*. New York, NY: Simon & Schuster Inc.

4) Margolis, M., (2009). *Believe Me: Why Your Vision, Brand, and Leadership Need a Bigger Story*. Retrieved from www.believemethebook.com

5) Dweck, C., (2006). *Mindset: The New Psychology of Success*. New York, NY: Random House.

6) Fredrickson, B., & Branigan, C., (2005). Positive emotions broaden the scope of attention and thought-action repertoires. *Cognition and Emotion*, 19, 313-332.

7) Lyubomirsky, S., (2008). *The How of Happiness: A Scientific Approach to Getting the Life You Want*. New York: Penguin Press.

8) Lyubomirsky, S., King, L., & Diener, E., (2005). The Benefits of Frequent Positive Affect: Does Happiness Lead to Success? *Psychological Bulletin, 131(6)*, 803-855.

9) Seligmen, M., (2011). *Flourish: A Visionary New Understanding of Happiness and Well-being*. New York, NY: Free Press.

10) Fredrickson, B., & Losada, M., (2005). Positive Affect and the Complex Dynamics of Human Flourishing. *American Psychologist, 60*, 678- 686.

11) Seligman, M., Steen, T., Park, N., & Peterson, C., (2005). Positive psychology progress: Empirical validation of interventions. *American Psychologist, 60*, 410-421.

12) Emmons, R., & McCullough, M., (2003). Counting Blessings Versus Burdens: An Experimental Investigation of Gratitude and Subjective Well-Being in Daily Life. *Journal of Personality, 84 (2)*, 377–389.

Chapter 11

1) Coyle, D., (2009). *The Talent Code*. New York, NY: Bantam Books.

2) Williams, J., Plassman, B., Burke, J., Holsinger, T., & Benjamin S., (April 2010). Preventing Alzheimer's Disease and Cognitive Decline. Evidence Report/ Technology Assessment No. 193. Rockville, MD: Agency for Healthcare Research and Quality.

3) Xu, W., Qui, C., Gatz, M., et al., (2009). Mid-and late-life diabetes in relation to the risk of dementia: a population-based twin study. *Diabetes, 58(1)*, 71-77.

4) Leider, R., (1997). *The Power of Purpose: Creating Meaning in Your Life and Work*. San Francisco, CA: Berrett-Koehler Publishers.

5) Buettner, D., (2008). *The Blue Zones: Lessons for Living Longer From the People Who've Lived the Longest*. Washington, DC: National Geographic Books.

6) Cousins, N., (2001). *Anatomy of an Illness as Perceived by the Patient: Reflections on Healing and Regeneration*. New York, NY: W. W. Norton & Company.

7) Field, T., Ironson, G., Scafidi, F., Nawrocki, T.,Goncalves, A., Burman, I. , Pickens, J., Fox, N., Schanberg, S., & Kuhn, C. (1996). Massage therapy reduces anxiety and enhances EEG pattern of alertness and math computations. *International Journal of Neuroscience, 86*, 197-205.

8) Hamilton, N.A., Kitzman, H., & Guyotte, S., (2006). Enhancing Health and Emotion: Mindfulness as a Missing Link Between Cognitive Therapy and Positive Psychology. *Journal of Cognitive Psychotherapy, 20* (2), 123-134.

9) Lambourne, K., & Tomporowski, P., (2010). The effect of exercise-induced arousal on cognitive task performance: A meta-regression analysis. *Brain Research: Exercise and the Brain, 1341*, 12-24.

10) Thompson, A., (2011). Healing the Western Mind through Yoga, in Yoga – Philosophy for Everyone: Bending Mind and Body (ed L. S. Swan), *Wiley-Blackwell*, Oxford, UK.

11) Tran, M.D., Holly, R.G., Lashbrook, J., & Amsterdam, E.A., (2001). Effects of Hatha Yoga Practice on the Health-Related Aspects of Physical Fitness. *Official Journal of the American Society for Preventative Cardiology, 4* (4), 165-170.

12) Smith, C., Hancock, H., Blake-Mortimer, J., & Eckert, K., (2007). A randomized comparative trial of yoga and relaxation to reduce stress and anxiety. *Complementary Therapies in Medicine, 15* (2), 77-83.

13) Ray, U.S., Sinha, B., Tomer, O.S., Pathak, A., Dasgupta, T., & Selvamurthy, W., (2001). Aerobic capacity & perceived exertion after practice of Hatha yogic exercises. *Indian J Med Res., 114*, 215-21.

14) Calajoe, A., (1986). Yoga as a therapeutic component in treating chemical dependency. *Alcoholism Treatment Quarterly, 3* (4), 33-46.

15) Carson, J.W., Carson, K.M., Porter, L.S., Keefe, F.J., Shaw, H., & Miller, J.M., (2007). Yoga for Women with Metastatic Breast Cancer: Results from a Pilot Study. *Journal of Pain and Symptom Management, 33* (3), 331-341.

16) Seligmen, M., Steen, T., Park, N., & Peterson, C., (2005). Positive Psychology Progress: Empirical Validation of Interventions. *American Psychologist, 60*, 410- 421.